PILGRIMAGE
from ROME

UNIVERSITY PRESS, INC.
Greenville, South Carolina 29614

Cover photo by Rex G. Salmon

Pilgrimage from Rome
by Bartholomew F. Brewer with Alfred W. Furrell

©1982 Bob Jones University Press, Inc.
Greenville, South Carolina 29614

Printed in the United States of America.

ISBN 0-89084-175-6

Dedicated to my beloved father and mother, who gave me a profound respect for the things of God; to my precious wife, Ruth, and son, Steven, whose love, patience, and long-suffering prompted me to write this book; and to Colonel Alfred

Introduction

There is a special burden on anyone, especially an ex-priest, who speaks or writes about the Church of Rome, for it is a vast and complex institution with many faces. It has a chameleon-like ability to adapt to almost any environment or condition, so it may be one thing in one country and something quite different in another. With equal ease it accommodates the diverse people of many lands, from presidents and princes of favored nations to the impoverished internees of leprosariums in Southeast Asia.

Over the centuries, a true church would have been a comfort and help to nations, communities, and individuals, for the teachings of the Bible show mankind not only his sin, but the way to salvation. The Bible gives counsel in solving economic, social, and even political problems. How tragic it is, then, that the Catholic church has been a major part of the problems of many nations, especially those of Latin America. Over and over, the Church of Rome has boldly hindered the education and progress of Catholic nations, preferring their ignorance and superstition to enlightenment, lest those whose eyes are opened to truth become a threat to the awesome power and wealth of the church.

Certainly the doctrines of Catholicism are not the teachings of our Lord Jesus Christ. Long ago it departed from following Christ, preferring false doctrines, pagan traditions, and corruption of truth to the revealed Word of God. The

Vatican knows this, scholars know it, and some priests know it. Still, the Catholic church would rather deceive the whole world than submit to the teachings of the Bible. It has bowed to the temptations of the evil one, and by deceptive reasoning, false traditions, and spurious additions to the Word, it presents "a form of godliness, but [denies] the power thereof" (II Timothy 3:5). Its palaces are rich, and its vestments are splendid: how different they are from those of the Son of God, Who had "not where to lay his head" (Matthew 8:20).

History teaches us that religious freedom is the basis of all other freedoms; those who would take away our civil liberties must also take away our religious liberties. History also proves that religious dictatorship can be every bit as repressive as political dictatorship. The Middle Ages were so terribly dominated by the Roman Church that millions of innocent persons were deprived of liberty and property, and hundreds of thousands were put to death for simply opposing wrongful practices of the church. Men and women were excommunicated for the flimsiest of reasons, and in those days excommunication was like being branded an outcast of the vilest form. The Catholic church even tried to keep the Bible from being printed in the common languages. In the early days of the Renaissance, the Bible was printed and distributed secretly, and many were martyred for reading and quoting Scripture. More Bibles have been burned by Catholic clerics than by atheists.

I willingly admit that if anyone had told me these things when I was a seminarian or a young priest, I would have been outraged; I would have run or plugged my ears. I would not have believed such charges and would have regarded them as authored by the Devil. I had been brainwashed against all such things. I was blind and under the tyrant's rod; but by the grace of God, my eyes were opened.

It is said that a child's basic character is formed by the time he is ten. How clearly I recall those early, happy years when I questioned nothing my parents and teachers told me. The tender years were sweet. I knew I was loved, and my happiness was dampened only by the untimely death of my beloved father.

I entered the seminary when I was 16 and applied myself diligently. Twelve years later I was ordained a Roman Catholic priest in the Discalced Carmelite Order. When I emerged, I did as I was told, wanting nothing more than to increase the church, desiring to live and die a Catholic priest, and perhaps even to become a saint.

I had been a priest about five years when a change began to come over my life. I was not at peace with either God or myself. So I worked harder, never entertaining a doubt about anything Catholic. I asked the Virgin for help, but peace eluded me. Oftentimes I felt that the wells of my soul were dry and the fruits of my labor were as grass. Though I could not reason why, I felt impatient when I listened to confessions, gave penances, and said mass. Sometimes I wondered what good I had done when I blessed such things as plaster figurines, tools, automobiles, and boats, or sprinkled holy water on baby cribs.

I began to question things I had once accepted. I searched the Scriptures for the foundations of my salvation; yet even in this I felt guilty, for I knew full well that such Bible study is discouraged by the church. Even priests are not permitted to make individual interpretations of Scripture that disagree with Rome.

What grief overcame me as I failed to find scriptural support for many things I believed and was teaching to others! Slowly I was compelled to accept a clear and awesome fact: many things taught by the Roman Catholic church are not in holy Scripture. Some teachings are mere inventions; some are adulterations of Christ's teachings. I saw that the rock of my salvation is not Peter, nor the church, nor the illustrious fathers, but that "that Rock was Christ," as the apostle Paul said (I Corinthians 10:4). I saw error, corruption, and delusion foisted on needy hearts. But in place of Catholicism's vast scheme of error, I found Jesus—the very same Who declared, "I am the way, the truth, and the life: no man cometh unto the Father, but by me" (John 14:6).

For this, I am anathema, a Judas, a renegade, a fugitive, and an apostate. My sin? I dared to search the Scriptures; and as a consequence, I stand excommunicated and condemned by the Catholic hierarchy to Hell's eternal fire.

This is the gospel of Rome.

Such condemnation is not the truth, however. I am not at enmity with God. I have wonderful peace and glory in my heart and soul, for I am redeemed through the blood of Jesus that was shed for me on Calvary. I am the servant of Him Who loved the world so much that He gave His only begotten Son, Jesus, to die on the cross and to rise from the tomb for our justification. I am eternally welcome to come directly to the throne of grace, not through any intermediary. I have no need of intercession by the Virgin Mary, the saints, popes, or priests. I have salvation for my soul through Him alone! I am free!

Now having experienced God's loving mercy and His forgiving grace, I must share the good news. I am determined not to know anything among you save Jesus Christ and Him crucified.

This is my testimony.

Alfred W. Furrell, born in 1911, grew up in Kansas City, Missouri, the oldest of seven children. He attended Pacific University and the University of Oregon where he was an R.O.T.C. cadet. He was commissioned a 2d lieutenant, Infantry, U.S. Army, and shortly after Pearl Harbor was called to active duty with the U.S. Army Air Force.

Later he was trained as an intelligence officer and assigned as Assistant Military Attache to India where he became acquainted with the late Mahatma Gandhi, Prime Minister Nehru, and Mohammed Ali Jinnah, the founder of modern Pakistan.

"It was during those years in India," he writes, "that I more clearly understood the glorious privileges and blessings that come from heralding the Word of God, and I found that the Army provided many opportunities. Even more, the words of the Apostle Paul were emblazoned on my heart as I witnessed the ills of the world: 'for there is none other name under heaven given among men, whereby we must be saved.' It became the chief spiritual motivation of my life."

Colonel Furrell and his wife, Dorothy, live in San Diego, California, where they work together writing on religious and historical subjects.

Contents

1 The Tender Years

I was about six or seven when Mother had an experience that meant much to her—an experience typical of Roman Catholics. She was bringing in a bundle from the clothesline and was about halfway up the stairs when she sensed a spiritual presence. As clearly as though someone was speaking to her, she heard the words: "I am your support." In shock, she stopped and answered, "But Lord, my husband is my support. This is his responsibility." Then came the quick reply, "No, I am your support. Whatever you need, ask Me and no one else."

Mother often told us this story with the conviction that although there were no audible words, it was a real experience with a lesson for our family. Two days after this incident, Father suffered a massive heart attack. Our doctor gave him a year to live.

Mother's poise upon learning this tragic news was remarkable. She felt that God had prepared her for this crisis. How many times we heard her repeat the text: "Take therefore no thought for the morrow: for the morrow shall take thought for the things of itself. Sufficient unto the day is the evil thereof" (Matthew 6:34).

At the suggestion of our family doctor, we moved to Stone Harbor, a southern New Jersey ocean resort. We moved into a large house with many windows and a large porch that offered an excellent view of the ocean on one side and the bay on the other. We lived in the north end of town; the parochial school was on the south side. So for a whole winter, cousin Tom and I missed school rather than attend the public school, which was practically around the corner from us. Life was slow and relaxed with a good bit of fishing and clamming with Dad and Mother. Most of our food came from the ocean.

Once we fished all day and caught nothing. But while we were walking home, a friend shouted, "Were you on the beach?" "No!" we shouted back; "We were fishing in the bay and got nothing." Our friend called back that there was a whole school of cod on the beach and that they were still alive! The result was that we had enough fish for a whole week.

God always met our needs in those depression years. My parents always thanked Him for His great provision and protection. Even though I was quite young, I was continually reminded of God's mercy and goodness. Down by the bay or the seashore, playing among the vernal pools left by the receding tide, I saw His handiwork in everything and learned a deep respect for all life.

One morning I decided to take the family rowboat out onto the bay for a ride. It seemed a harmless thing to do. But I had not rowed very far from shore when I was caught in a fast current. I tried to get back to shore, but the current became stronger and faster, carrying me far out onto the bay toward the open sea just beyond the drawbridge. I rowed hard and prayed for the help and guidance that I thought God always provided the Brewer family. My situation became more perilous with each passing moment with the waves rising and lapping over into my boat. As I came to the drawbridge and the swells began to turn my boat from side to side, I called for help although I saw no one and even the drawbridge was vacant. At the last moment a man on shore saw my little craft bobbing toward the ocean. Frantically he searched the shore until he found a boat, which he cut loose and rowed out to rescue me. Later he told me that I was so far out that he wasn't sure he was seeing a boat. A little farther and the great Atlantic Ocean would have engulfed me. God and a brave and noble man saved the day for me. I could not help feeling that

God had a special purpose in saving my life.

Instead of improving, Dad grew steadily worse. The heavy salt air didn't agree with him, and the doctor told us to move away from the coast. Since there was very little income, the need for finding a house at a price we could afford was of great concern to Mother. A few days after the doctor told us to move, Mother had a dream in which she saw a house. When a family friend offered to help her find a house, she related her dream to him. He told her that he had heard of a place in Magnolia, New Jersey, that might be within our means. He took us to see it. Even as we stopped in front of the house, Mother exclaimed that it was the one she had seen in her dream. How grateful we were! We felt we were safe in the hands of God.

My brother, Paul, was born in December of the year that we moved into this house. Somehow his birth just a week before Christmas seemed like a very special Christmas present. It made the birth of Jesus very real and meaningful to us.

Dad must have known that this was his last Christmas. He did everything humanly possible to make the day unforgettable. There was a huge tree from the northern New Jersey forests and many gifts around its base. There were many toys that Dad had laboriously made for me and my cousin Tom, who had come to live with us. Despite his pain, Dad showed us how each toy worked, laughing as we delightedly pushed the wooden toys across the floor. He made it a memorable day for us all. Even Ruby, our Boston terrier, got a few gifts. Yet the greatest gift of all was my new baby brother, with his golden hair, blue eyes, and fair complexion. Dad went downhill fast after that and passed away a few months later. Mother said that God gave us Paul because He knew Dad would pass away. He was thirty-eight, and his last words to Mother were, "Catherine, tell the boys never to make war and never to smoke."

Now that Father was gone, Tom and I felt a sense of responsibility in helping Mother. She encouraged us to pray for Dad, and we did—just in case he was in the torment of purgatory. His goodness to us, his mild disposition, and his love for Mother made it difficult for us to believe that he was suffering punishment. Every day we threw kisses heavenward. I felt certain that he was there waiting for us.

With Dad gone, there wasn't much need for a three-bedroom house, so we moved to a much smaller house in Magnolia. Our neighbors were Protestants, the belligerent kind who threw stones at our house, bullied Tom and me, and called us "cat-licks." We couldn't understand why they hated us so. Mother could make no friends in the neighborhood, so we moved again—this time to Somerdale, not far away. It was a welcome relief to learn that our new neighbors were Irish and Italian Catholics. In a sense it was ironic, for our house was a remodeled Presbyterian church that had been abandoned several years before. Our rent was only three dollars per month.

The Catholic church in Somerdale was a mission, having mass only on Sundays. The nearest Catholic school, St. Lawrence, was in Laurel Springs. Paul wasn't old enough for school, but Tom and I resolved to attend the Catholic school four miles away, rather than the public school nearby. There were many days when the snows were deep and the school bus didn't show up, but we took work home and managed to keep up with the class.

It was at St. Lawrence that the Dominican sisters taught us to cultivate the habit of making daily visits to the Blessed Sacrament, which is the consecrated host or wafer used in the mass. During the lunch hour I would kneel before the altar and pray to Jesus in the tabernacle. I felt a mystical union with Christ, a personal identification with Him. More and more, He became real to me; later on, when I was a seminarian, the Blessed Sacrament meant much to me. I would repeat the words, *"Adoro te devote, latens Deitas, Quae sub his figuris vere latitas . . . ."* ("I adore thee, O unseen God, Who under these external signs [of bread and wine] art truly hidden. . . .")[1]

We made many friends in Somerdale and at school and

---

[1]Joseph Connelly, ed., *Hymns of the Roman Liturgy* (Westminster, MD: Newman, 1957), p. 128.

in church at Laurel Springs. The Dominican sisters who ran St. Lawrence were especially good to our family, oftentimes making small items of clothing for us and baking oatmeal cookies for the holidays. We hated to leave our Irish and Italian friends, but we had to move again—this time to Philadelphia to be nearer my Aunt Mary, a physician, who was a great help to us.

We moved to 1806 Green Street, next door to a Dominican convent. Before long, Mother and the nuns developed a close relationship. The nuns were impressed with Mother's devotion. A family that attended daily mass, weekly confession, the daily recitation of the rosary, and veneration for every Catholic priest and nun aroused their interest and admiration.

Frankly, I had never entertained the idea of becoming a priest. But after seeing a few films about priests—*Boys' Town* and others—I thought to myself how wonderful it would be to serve God and man this way. At school, church, and home we heard about the glory of the priesthood and the heroic lives that priests led for the Lord. The Roman priesthood was described as the most desirable, the most honored, and the most respected of all callings. However, such a calling seemed far beyond me, for I felt myself too ordinary for such honor. The more I thought about the priesthood, the more I tried to dismiss the idea as arrogant and presumptuous.

The sisters next door watched me. They told Mother they were praying that I would be a priest. Frequently they gave me holy cards with special prayers for those called to the priesthood. Sometimes they dropped hints that I looked like a priest, walked like a priest, and talked like a priest. Sister Catherine, an intimate friend of Mother, often said that God was calling me to the priestly state. They did the same thing to Paul, who at this time was only five years old. Some of them would say to him, "Father Paul, Father Paul, would you hear our confession?"

Then it happened. Our favorite nun, who happened to be the prettiest, was paid a visit by her brother, Edward, who was home from the Discalced Carmelite Seminary at Holy Hill, near Hartford, Wisconsin, where he was a student. Several sisters asked me to meet the seminarian, who also wanted to meet me. I was thrilled as he told me about the glories of life in the seminary and the illustrious history of the Carmelite order. Although it was a short visit, I was thrilled when he said, "Why don't you go to Holy Hill with me in September? You can be a priest too!" A few days later I announced to Mother that God wanted me to be His priest—Christ's alter ego among men.

That was June. With fear and trembling I applied for entrance into the seminary. The glory and wonder of it all were magnified to me when I was accepted by the father rector. Mother spent her last few dollars to buy my first suit and clothing suitable for the long Wisconsin winter. Friends at the Cathedral of Saints Peter and Paul, friends at the Divine Love Chapel, and friends at the convent next door generously helped our family and prepared me for the seminary. Monsignor Hubert Cartwright was especially helpful, encouraging me and making sure that our daily needs were met. In early September, Edward and I took the train from North Philadelphia for Holy Hill.

Life would never be the same.

2 The Greenhouse

Holy Hill is a place of breathtaking beauty and panoramic view. It is advertised as America's favorite place of pilgrimage where thousands every year visit to pay homage to "Mary, Help of Christians," as the shrine is called. More than a hundred years ago, rugged Bavarian Carmelite monks left the security of their homeland to found this picturesque place as a haven of contemplation.

The first time I saw my future home, chills went up and down my spine. The medley of autumn colors set the countryside ablaze. I had never seen anything like this before. My heart pounded with excitement as the train stopped at a well-known view point. Seven apple-cheeked seminarians pointed out to me the two celebrated spires that pierced the blue, smogless Wisconsin sky. On the distant horizon stood the imposing edifice in traditional European grandeur. As I feasted my eyes on the scene, a surety came over me that God would grant me the gift of perseverance: that I would complete my first four years before entering the monastery.

"Why shouldn't I succeed?" I asked myself. The Dominican nuns on Green Street were praying for me; so were the Pink sisters back home on 22nd Street. The sisters at St. Lawrence school in Laurel Springs and the sisters at the Cathedral of Saints Peter and Paul were praying for their little "Freddie." Then there was the encouragement of my pastor, Monsignor Cartwright. And more than this, there were the love, devotion, prayers, and sacrifices of Mother. Though she never called my leaving home a sacrifice, I knew it was; the older of the two boys, I could have been expected to take over special responsibilities for the family.

When the train arrived at the depot in Hartford, I saw a small man with a warm smile standing on the platform. It was Father Louis Clarke, the father rector of the seminary, clad in the brown habit and sandals of the Discalced Carmelite order. I guess it was the impatience of youth that made me long for the day when I would wear the same religious habit.

With suitcases and trunks piled into an old 1941 Ford pickup and our skinny bodies squeezed into a nearby car, we were off!

My friend Ed, who first encouraged me to try the seminary, had told me that it was a beautiful place, but I never dreamed that it was this beautiful. Interspersed amid a wooded setting were a gigantic brick monastery, seminary, guest house, souvenir store, refreshment stand, and challenging serpentine pathway winding gracefully along fourteen life-size Stations of the Cross. From the top of the hill, where everything was enormous and impressive, I felt separated from what seemed to be a miniature and distant world outside.

The word "seminary" comes from the Latin *seminarium,* meaning "seed-plot." Candidates for the priesthood are set apart from the world "from their tender years," before the pages of the heart are inscribed with too many other experiences and teachings. In the controlled, clerical environment, candidates are insulated from the distracting influences of the outside world, and priestly vocations are nurtured. It is a "greenhouse" of harmony, discipline, respect, and devotion.

The average day was long and busy. Bells ran my life from sunrise to sundown. A wooden clapper woke everyone at 5:30. We had thirty minutes to get ourselves together before going to the chapel, where we donned cassocks for mass. Like most Roman Catholics I didn't understand the true doctrine or theology of the mass, yet I loved it. I could hardly wait each day to attend mass, to serve the mass as an acolyte. I was so deeply moved by devotion and yearnings that I developed a strong desire to be God's best seminarian! I think the one thing I prayed for most was obedience. I knew that if I were obedient, I would make it to the priesthood.

I never had any problem answering the call to breakfast. We young fellows ate with plenty of gusto. We knew that we would spend most of the day in the classroom, trying to master Latin and other subjects. I was far from a straight A student, but I was always proud of my A's in Conduct and Personal Application.

By late morning we teenagers were ravenously hungry, and it was time for another trip to the refectory, which was similar to a cafeteria. A continuous bench lined three walls of the large room, where we sat according to seniority on two sides. At the head tables were the father rector and sometimes a visiting priest. At the opposite end of the room was a lectern, from which throughout the meal a book was read, such as *The Greatest Story Ever Told* or *Ben Hur*. These were times I dreaded, because whenever the reader made a mistake, the rector would signal by tapping on his cup with his knife. If I was the reader, I would blush with embarrassment and perhaps stumble again, but he was patient and gentle. Obviously, there was missing the clatter and clang characteristic of normal school campuses. But this was a great bunch of kids, serious about the seminary.

Classwork was over by three—time to unwind and relax by playing ball or other sports. Then study hall, communal prayers, dinner, recreation, and evening prayers before retiring. Before rising and retiring, I always kissed the Carmelite brown scapular that I wore to bed. All of us wore one to bed to get a five-hundred-day indulgence and to claim the promise of the Virgin Mary to Saint Simon Stock that "he who dies in this habit shall be saved."

Now, these seminarians were not running away from jail, the army, or mother's apron strings. They were not maladjusted youths or rebels. No! Quite the opposite: they were an idealistic bunch of sparkling-eyed boys from the big cities, small towns, and farming communities of America, who wanted to serve God, their church, and the people. I don't know of one student who was there against his will.

Entering the seminary didn't represent "social suicide." Though the seminary did stifle personality development, foster immaturity, and even create problems in sexual identification, such things did not seem threats to any of us, so far as I know. Young boys and girls are recruited early in life, when zeal and idealism are powerful; nevertheless, we weren't ignorant of what we were getting into. Nor did our motives go unchallenged. No one failed to tell us that the celibate state is against nature. Often we were told of the chastisement that befalls sinful priests. Distractions were few, and to us, the whole world of the church was as we were. We did not wince or cry aloud even at the rigorous discipline, nor did we even think of ourselves as making any special sacrifice. There was a prize at the end of our journey—to be ordained as God's priests; and I, for one, welcomed the discipline and the serenity that prize bestowed.

Priests were called by St. Prosper of Aquitain "dispensers in the royal house." We were told that God chooses priests from among millions of young men so that they may be His own ministers, who are privileged to offer to Him, in sacrifice, His very own Son! We read books such as *The Faith of Millions* by John A. O'Brien, who explains that Christ is brought down from Heaven by the priest and presented as the victim of man's sins. We were told that when the priest speaks, God bows His head in humble obedience to his command. The awful arrogance of such teachings that would place a priest above the omnipotent God did not seem wrong to me at the time. In my eyes, these teachings exalted the status of the priest, who at a certain moment in the mass could command the obedience of God Himself. We were proud and felt lifted above all mortals of the earth as we learned that God has given the priest power over the very body of Jesus Christ. We were told that God has placed in the priest's hands the keys to paradise; He has raised the priest above all the kings of the earth and above all the angels of Heaven. We were told that the priest is like God Himself as he performs his earthly ministry. I observed that it gave to some a sense of omnipotence, of subjection to no one save their superiors in the church. One Catholic publication says, "If I were to meet a priest and an angel, I would salute the priest before saluting the angel. The priest holds the place of God."[2]

Our young, eager hearts and minds questioned not a thing. We dared not! Obedience to church doctrine and our superiors came from the very core of our young hearts and souls. To question the church was to question God. It was unthinkable! Moreover, anyone who questioned or expressed a doubt never reached ordination! Thus, as we moved through the spiritual desert toward ordination, the driving sands of false doctrine and ancient tradition blinded us.

Never mind that the Bible says, "For in that he died, he died unto sin once: but in that he liveth, he liveth unto God" (Romans 6:10). Never mind that Jesus, "knowing that all things were now accomplished, . . . said, It is finished" (John 19:28, 30), or that the writer to the Hebrews said, "Every priest standeth daily ministering and offering oftentimes the same sacrifices, which can never take away sins: But this man [Jesus], after he had offered one sacrifice for sins for ever, sat down on the right hand of God" (10:11,12).

It was much later in my life that I saw that Jesus completed the work of redemption by His death on the cross. He bridged the gulf by His substitutionary death and gave a clear title of forgiveness to all those who believe and receive Him; and when He arose from the grave, He justified us freely forever. How, then, can anyone claim that Christ is again offered as a sacrifice in the mass? It is to be abhorred as an adulteration of Scripture. Its purpose, quite clearly, is to bestow on the church and the priest an awesome power over the church's subjects.

We were not allowed to know, even in the slightest detail, that Roman Catholic priestcraft is contrary to Scripture; for church doctrine and the writings of ancient fathers and popes are held superior to Scripture. Nor could we see the incredible subtlety of such teachings, for they keep millions of devout Catholics in bondage, always anxious lest the avenging sword of God's wrath fall upon their heads. Obedience thus becomes

---

[2]Quoted by Loraine Boettner, *Roman Catholicism* (Philadelphia: Presbyterian and Reformed, 1962), p. 51.

paramount. The devout Catholic who sins or stumbles looks to the priest for forgiveness. Thus the power of the church and priests over penitent Catholics is beyond imagination. Nor does it stop at death; Catholics are taught that they must implore the priest and seek the help of the Virgin Mary and the saints to rescue them from the sufferings of purgatory.

No! I questioned nothing I was told to do nor anything I was taught.

When I entered the seminary, I took it for granted that I would be there for good. I knew that it was not easy to become a seminarian and later a priest, but I never gave it a thought that anyone would quit the seminary. It didn't take me long, however, to realize how wrong I was. The long years of hard study, prayer, and discipline in the seminary and the monastery separated the men from the boys, the weak from the strong, the committed from the uncommitted. Those who did poorly in their studies or who couldn't adjust to seminary life, those who had health or sexual problems or were maladjusted, were dropped. Yet every time a student left the seminary, it offended me. It was like a rejection of God and His church. To me it smacked of the sin of unbelief: there was no room for weakness, and while I always felt sorry for the quitters, I looked down my nose at them.

My attitude on that has changed. I admire some of those who left the seminary, for I realize that in some cases it took more courage to leave than to stay. Yet in another sense, I feel sorry for them, not because they never became priests, but because they clung to an unrealistic image of what a priest really is. Only God knows how many former seminarians, former priests, and former nuns go through life in despair, burdened with guilt and fear, feeling that every adversity and pain is God's punishment. Oftentimes they are ostracized and persecuted by friends and relatives. Many regard themselves as thrice failures: failures to God, failures to family and friends, and failures to themselves! Unprepared for the realities of daily life, having given up the past and security, sometimes emotionally crippled, how can they start anew?

Our indoctrination in the seminary was remarkable, born as it was of centuries of practice and skill. We eagerly anticipated the joys and privileges of increasing the Roman Church's power, prestige, and pageantry. The time flew. Classwork, discussions, and sports were interesting, but the highlight of each year was the fall retreat—a full week off from schoolwork, a week of stimulating messages by some retreat master who came to Holy Hill from Chicago or Milwaukee, or even from overseas. My favorite retreat was given by a Jesuit from Marquette University. I think his name was Maddigan. Not only were his talks alive and relevant, but they were "spiritual." Prayer, eternal chastity, charity, obedience, and devotion to Mary and the priesthood were all covered. After the retreat Father Maddigan gave each of us a little plaque upon which he had personally written the words, "I wish, I can, I will." That little plaque stood on my desk for the next eleven years. Every morning I ritualistically chanted these words until the day Bishop McNamara of Washington, D.C., laid his hands on my head and said I was "a priest forever after the Order of Melchisedec." Rome's exaggerated emphasis on perseverance had much to do with my going all the way, so committed to that goal that nothing else really mattered.

The exemplary life-style of the Discalced Carmelite Fathers who guided and nurtured us young aspirants during those formative years had a hypnotic influence on us. They persuaded us not to count the cost, not to deviate from the path leading to the priesthood. From the very beginning, my enthusiasm to be a priest was noticeable to professors and students alike. The rector singled me out as one definitely chosen by God to be "in the person of Christ."[3] I can truthfully say that I never doubted my calling to be a priest from the day I entered the seminary.

Life wasn't all that serious, however. I shall never forget the time I was literally caught with my pants down! A fellow seminarian and I were hurrying to change our clothes for a baseball game when in walked one of the students with his

---

[3]Pope Pius XII, quoted by Karl Rahner, S.J., ed., *The Teaching of the Catholic Church,* trans. Geoffrey Stevens (Staten Island: Alba House, 1967), p. 349.

two sisters, one on each arm. Stripped down as we were, there was no time to run for cover. With flushed, cherubic faces we simply sat down on our beds, snickered a little, and breathed a prayer that the intruders might "buzz off."

Then there were the days of the plain T-shirts. Casual dress was allowed for the classroom; however, a few of us from Philadelphia couldn't be bothered to slip on another shirt for chapel services each evening. One day the father rector decided that he had had enough of this inappropriate attire. Kindly but firmly he told us that in the future we were to wear ties to chapel. Ah! Someone had a bright idea. I think it was Johnny Miller, later known as Father Gregory Miller, who eventually left the priesthood. We would do exactly as we were told. The next morning four of us sat religiously and boldly in our assigned places, still wearing our soft white T-shirts, our ties carefully knotted—not under stiff collars, but around our bare necks. The reaction was hilarious laughter. It was a great day for our little joke, but we acted very solemn and penitent as the rector patiently explained that ties and T-shirts do not mix.

My only real reprimand concerned my attitude toward sports. The baseball and football seasons became occasions of much competition. Those who didn't excel in athletics, to my way of thinking, either were deficient in some way or didn't have a call to the priesthood. I remember how in my first year at the "Sem," those of us who liked sports downright persecuted those who did not. It reached such a point that the rector had to put a stop to it. One day he called me into his office to tell me that I was making a god out of athletics. He was right. I knew that. "Playing ball," he said, "is only a means to an end. You are not in the seminary to become a professional ball player, but rather to become a professional priest for God." Everyone, young and old, strays from the straight path now and then, and at such times he needs a gentle tap, or sometimes a firm one, to put him back on the track.

Though I was overly serious about sports, I was just as serious about my studies. Lots of hard work, with long hours of hitting the books and memorizing to make the grade, characterized my life. I was a plugger. Several times I even requested special permission to rise an hour early to put in extra study for examinations. I felt that I needed everything I could learn and every help the church could provide if I were to be the perfect priest. It was because of this that I had been advised to apply myself more to sports. I overdid that too.

I don't recall any dull moments "on the Hill." Life was full of interesting things to learn and to do. It was mysterious and beautiful even when death struck. When dear old Father Augustine died, there was no sadness. Instead there was great rejoicing throughout the seminary and monastery, not because he had died, but because of his long and faithful years of service to Christ's church and to Mary's order. Dying with the brown scapular around his neck, having the last rites of the church, surrounded by the religious community he loved—that was the ultimate. "What a way to go!" said one monk as we reviewed his life of service.

Father Augustine's body was laid in state in the church. Dressed in full religious garb with the priestly stole, he seemed to be God's representative, sharing in the priesthood of Jesus Christ. Tall candles surrounded his casket and flickered in the darkness, and in the shadows of night one could sense an eerie atmosphere, especially while the cold winter winds howled outside. Different seminarians kept vigil beside the corpse. When it came my turn to keep vigil, I meditated on the shortness of life: "As for man, his days are as grass: as a flower of the field, so he flourisheth. For the wind passeth over it, and it is gone; and the place thereof shall know it no more. But the mercy of the Lord is from everlasting to everlasting upon them that fear him, and his righteousness unto children's children" (Psalm 103:15-17).

Of course I prayed for the repose of his soul, for it was assumed that he was in purgatory. And though none of us knew anything about the nature or duration of purgatory, we prayed that his time would be short. The next morning, after the Requiem High Mass, Father Augustine was buried behind the seventh Station of the Cross in the cold, hard earth of January, and I prayed that someday I, too, would die a Carmelite.

The old friar's spirit, so the rector told us, was seen near the chapel entrance. Now, up to that time, I had always enjoyed slipping into the chapel every evening to pray before the altar. For me, Christ was in that golden tabernacle. That is why, before leaving the chapel, I would go up to the tabernacle in fear and trembling to touch it, out of respect for Christ's "real" presence; I felt that it brought me closer to God, that it would energize my whole being and make me a great son of the church and a priest after God's own heart. But after hearing of the deceased friar's appearing outside the chapel door, I never again went to the chapel alone at night. I was afraid that I might encounter his ghost, and if I did, what would I do? What would I say? Or worse, what would he do or say?

I think it was then that I first realized how little I knew about life after death and the mysteries of eternity. But I was not afraid, for I felt that a complete knowledge of truth and a full assurance of salvation would come later. I began to wonder why the living are so unaware of death, since it must come to every man and woman.

It is incredible how time flew during seminary days. The fall months were followed by the winter, and winter by spring; before we knew it, it was time to go home for the summer months. My heart leaped with joy as I thought of seeing Mother and Paul again and taking long walks through Fairmount Park, not far from where we lived. I looked forward to attending mass again at the Cathedral of Saints Peter and Paul and, perhaps, seeing the A's or the Phillies play ball.

I shall never forget that first summer at home from the seminary. I worked as a busboy at the cafeteria in the main post office in Philadelphia. The difference between life on the hill and life in the world was like that between night and day. The vulgarity and immorality of two Roman Catholic men at work made me appreciate my vocation to the priesthood and religious life. These men believed that my innocence concerning women was depriving me of the normal sexual outlets that young men have. They mounted a campaign geared to break down my resistance to the world, the flesh, and the

Devil, but we had been warned against these things.

Dating during the summer months often destroyed a boy's dream of being a priest. I didn't want that to happen to me; and though marriage is said to be a sacrament, the father rector did a good job of putting marriage down by saying that most women after five or ten years of marriage become ugly, fat, and domineering. We were led to believe that love is a lure that destroys both priestly vows and chastity, and the glories of virginity were magnified. Butler's *Lives of the Saints* provided an example of Roman saints who would rather sacrifice their lives than defile their bodies with impurity. In the seminary chapel and in the large church atop the hill there were statues of the Virgin Mary and St. Joseph, each with a lily in hand. St. Agatha and St. Anthony were virgins, according to the Catholic legend. Rarely did we hear anything about the Roman saints who had families. Such fear had been instilled into me that I resolved not to date. Still, I had a lot of trouble mortifying my eyes; hence, every Saturday afternoon I would run to confession and tell the priest of my inability to control my eyes. The confessor told me to pray to Mary and to say the rosary, and suggested that I keep a rosary in each pocket as a protection against impurity. I did, and I thought it helped.

I did not know why the vow of celibacy is so important to the Roman Catholic church. Now, of course, the church's prohibition against marriage is easy to understand. Marriage is natural; celibacy is unnatural and claims its penalties. The nature of marriage tends to diminish Rome's centralized authority. It dilutes the authority of superiors and can involve legal entanglements over property, especially at death. In those cases where church doctrine runs contrary to common sense, equity, or law, a wife's influence might often be greater than that of the church. Some married priests might be compelled to make a choice between family and the priesthood. Obviously, the vow of celibacy tends to guarantee the priest's insulation from the world of reality where there are love and mundane cares, such as shopping, house repairs, children, and schoolbooks. Studies have shown that celibacy frequently causes great emotional and mental problems; one wonders how the priest can effectively counsel men and women on the marriage problems that are common today. He can hardly understand the problems, for he has not experienced the heartaches that make a couple think that divorce is the only way out of their difficulties. Bad advice, such as sexual abstinence, has turned husbands and wives against each other and both against the church.

While I had been away at the seminary, my brother, Paul, had become so caught up in religious things that by the age of six he was "playing mass." That summer he would put on Mother's long, dark robe, and I had to be his altar boy, with the family dresser serving as his altar. Oftentimes he paraded up and down our yard next to the convent, chanting certain parts of the mass and an old Latin hymn for benediction of the Blessed Sacrament, *Tantum Ergo Sacramentum* (For So Great a Sacrifice). The Dominican nuns were amazed at Paul's ability to memorize certain parts of the mass and to master so much Latin just by hearsay. They often told Mother how much they enjoyed watching him from their windows; they not infrequently shouted, "Hello, Father Paul." Ten years later he entered the seminary at Holy Hill, only to learn later that it wasn't his calling.

As much as I enjoyed my responsibilities at home, I couldn't forget Holy Hill. I begged the rector to allow me to return a month early. He did, giving me work around the premises. I always felt guilty about leaving home earlier to indulge in the beauty of the place, because I'm sure that I hurt my mother and brother, even though they said nothing.

World War II started just a few months after I entered the seminary. Some seminarians left the hill to fight for their country, but a good percentage stayed. Insulated from the world as we were, having no radios or newspapers, we were not kept up on the news. Letters from relatives told us of major events, and from time to time a letter came telling of a student's father or brother lost in the war. Then the war would seem very close, and a wave of grief would sweep over Holy Hill. More would talk of leaving to enlist in the military services, and on several occasions it appeared that the student body would be decimated. But we worked, studied, and prayed, believing this to be our best duty toward God and country.

Toward the end of my fourth year in the minor seminary, the war was coming to an end. I was ready to enter the novitiate.

The summer of 1945 seemed long. The days, weeks, and months dragged on until I got word that I was to enter the novitiate in Brookline, Massachusetts, at a large ivy-covered mansion on Warren Road, just up from Jamaica Pond and a few miles from Boston College.

There wasn't any weeping or gnashing of teeth when I finally said good-bye to Mother and Paul, not to return home for eight years as a priest. I had been gone long enough that the family had learned to adjust to my absence. I was loved but not missed as much as before. Moreover, we firmly felt that this was God's will, God's call, sacred and unquestionable. I knew there would be loneliness, poverty, silence, manual labor, hard studies, and little sleep. I looked forward to the times of prayer, fasting, and abstinence from worldly pleasures like movies, parties, visits of friends, and sporting events. I knew that monastic life makes West Point look like a Sunday school picnic; but that didn't frighten me in the least, because God's grace was something always emphasized in our family, and now, if ever, was the time to apply it!

3 "I Wish, I Can, I Will"

In August 1945 I arrived at 514 Warren Road, Brookline, Massachusetts. It was to be my home for the next two years. There I was stripped of all independent thought, individual expression, and creativity. Implicit obedience of body and mind was the order of the day; uniformity was the objective. This was the life I cheerfully embraced because I believed that my religious superior in the monastery was a Christ on earth, before whose command my own will must be canceled. I knew life would not be easy, but I was ready. I had been prepared at home, at school, and in the seminary.

I do not wish to imply that it was a dreary or morbid place. Nor was it a world peopled with dour-faced, brown-robed men who trudged in sad contemplation through long, cold, vaulted corridors. Quite to the contrary, they were eager young men, and most of our superiors were zealous and dedicated in fulfilling their mission. Every waking hour had its occupation.

I was given an eight-by-twelve-foot cell furnished with a hard plywood bed and thin mat, a locker, a desk, a chair, and a simple cross hanging on the wall. The cross had no corpus (image), meaning that as a novice I was to find Christ for myself wherever He might be and, I must add, without use of holy Scriptures.

The isolated refuge of such a monastery may be likened to a secret kingdom whose high walls mute the realities of daily life. Thus sequestered, we were fitted into a pattern of monastic life. We lost touch with the world and with friends, and it was not long until we were only dimly aware of the passing scenes in the outside world. I look back in astonishment at how our young Catholic minds were shaped and honed to complete uniformity in thought and action. I would not have thought it possible to shape the human mind and spirit like a potter molding clay vessels. But it is. This shaping did not seem to be skillful manipulation; it seemed as natural as breathing. Distractions from the outside were kept to a minimum. Visits by friends and relatives were permitted only in cases of emergency. Newspapers, magazines, and radio were zealously forbidden. Even the library was off-limits without special permission, and the Bible was treated as a closed book.

Now, looking back, I marvel at the effects that were achieved. For in this guarded environment we were remade, even though it had a chilling effect on both our emotions and intellect. We quickly learned that we should question nothing we were taught. We became stoic, subduing our feelings to the disciplines of the order. Therefore, deep draughts of sorrow or joy seldom entered the cloistered halls. There was contentment without contention. We were placid, calm, submissive, and easily impressed.

We also considered such an experience the ultimate privilege. How else could anyone aspire to such a high calling? We, who would become priests, believed we were being prepared to become intercessors between God and man. We were spiritual guardians and "dispensers in the royal house" with God-like authority, even in matters of life and death.

Our claims to such authority were not mere assumptions. They rested on holy dogma. In 1546, the Council of Trent had declared Catholic tradition equal with holy Scripture. As time rolled by, it supplanted and oftentimes was made superior to the Word of God. The council's decrees were declared to be sacred, infallible doctrine, and the church required that they be accepted. Disobedience to or rejection of the council's decrees was declared a mortal sin that could result in excommunication. The council said, "The priest is a man of God, the minister of God. He that despiseth the priest despiseth God; he that hears him hears God. The priest remits sin as God, and that which he calls His body at the altar is adored as God by himself and by the congregation. It is clear that their function is such that none greater can be conceived. Wherefore, they are justly called not only angels but also God, holding as they do among us, the powers and authority of immortal God."[4]

St. John Vianney of France wrote, "Where there is no priest, there is no sacrifice; and where there is no sacrifice, there is no religion. Without the priest, the death and passion of our Lord would be of no avail. See the power of the priest! By one word from his lips he changes a piece of bread into a God! a greater feat than the creation of the world."

With zeal, therefore, we immersed ourselves in the teachings of saints and Carmelite traditions. Contemplative prayer put into action is the Carmelite's way of fulfilling his calling. As a Discalced (barefooted) Carmelite, I tried to live and work in apostolic commitment to Him, to my brother Carmelites, and to the world.

I was thrilled when, soon after I arrived, I was invested with the habit of the order, for at that time I also took a new name symbolic of death to my old life and the genesis of a new life. I chose Bartholomew because I was fascinated by the legends about the holiness and dedication of this apostle, who is said to have been martyred by being skinned alive and decapitated.

There was also a second name to be taken, one representing some mystery, such as the Incarnation, the Holy Rosary, the Infant Jesus of Prague, and others. I chose the Holy Spirit because I needed help. I was then Brother Bartholomew of the Holy Spirit until ordination, when I became Father Bartholomew.

Tradition says that the Carmelite order is of very ancient origin. For centuries, groups of men have lived together in monasteries, sometimes in caves, sometimes in the forests or in the deserts: the Hindus of India; the Essenes, an ancient Jewish sect of ascetics; and later the followers of Gautama

[4]Boettner, p. 51.

Buddha of India. The Carmelites took their name from
Mount Carmel in Palestine, where the Old Testament
prophet Elijah is said to have practiced monasticism nearly
nine centuries before Christ. It is said that since that time
there has been an unbroken chain of holy men living on or
near Mount Carmel.

The Carmelites multiplied and spread throughout the
world; today many of them are called "saints," "blesseds,"
and "venerables." In keeping with their motto, "With zeal
have I been zealous for the Lord God of Hosts," the
Carmelites have endeavored to be first among all. Before the
Second Vatican Council of Pope John XXIII, the Discalced
Carmelite order was one of the strictest. Its traditions and
superstitions are old, colorful, and appealing to the ascetic
mind. The scapular is an example. This small strip of cloth,
worn around the neck and shoulders, is said to have been
presented by the Virgin Mary to Saint Simon Stock in the
thirteenth century. In the presence of a multitude of angels,
Mary said, "This shall be a privilege unto thee and all
Carmelites; he who dies in this habit shall be saved."[5] This
indulgence, known as the Sabbatine Privilege and endorsed
by several popes, is known to be a mere invention. Yet many
of the pious firmly believe that this scapular will save from
Hell any Carmelite who wears it till death and that it will
deliver the soul from purgatory, at least on the first Saturday
following the Carmelite's death. According to ancient
tradition, Saturday is the Virgin Mary's day.

Like most other orders, the Carmelites became deplor-
ably corrupt and lax in discipline in the Middle Ages. Then a
chivalrous nun, St. Teresa of Avila—the first female doctor of
the church—and a mystic monk, St. John of the Cross, both
from Spain, set out to reform the Carmelite order. Though
Teresa endured incredible hardships and opposition within
the church itself, she succeeded in forming the Discalced
Carmelites in the sixteenth century. To this day the order's
primary emphasis is on contemplation, a kind of monastic life

---

[5]Herbert Thurston, S.J., and Donald Attwater, *Butler's Lives of the Saints* (New York: P. S. Kenedy & Sons, 1956), II, p. 331.

considered by many the way, par excellence, to heaven. Then from Lisieux, France, there came Saint Therese (Little Flower), who lived in poverty. She set an example of detachment from the pleasures of the senses. She spent hours in mental prayer with intense commitment to self-atonement through physical suffering. That meant much to me, a young novice. My heart went out to her. It was the Little Flower that I loved. I was proud to be a Carmelite and to be like her.

Catholics have always considered external unity to be one of the marks of God's true church, but there were times during my preordination years that I was astonished by the crusadelike rivalry—jealousy, pride and shameless enmity—among the various religious orders. It was said that the Dominicans have all the money and a fierce reputation for the ways in which they acquired some of it. The Jesuits are the intellectuals; the Franciscans have great pride in their humility. The Trappists are the regimented farmers, while the Calced Carmelites, unlike the Discalced Carmelites, indulge in wearing shoes and eating meat. To us, members of all other religious orders and congregations, such as the Paulist Fathers and the Josephites, were second-rate citizens.

I was determined to be a true Carmelite. I stirred myself to follow all the rigors of monastic life, endeavoring to crucify my flesh by fastings, mortifications, and vigils. Self-punishment and self-abnegation were an integral part of the Carmelite routine. Though I knew nothing about Martin Luther at the time, I could have said, as he once did, "I was a good monk, and I kept the rule of my order so strictly that I may say that if ever a monk got to heaven by his monkery it was I. All my brothers in the monastery who knew me will bear me out."[6]

I was trying with all my strength to earn my salvation. Yet the more I tried, the less certain I became. My faith was in church dogma, which I believed was synonymous with the Word of God. I knew nothing of the Epistle to the Ephesians, wherein Paul wrote, "For by grace are ye saved through faith;

---

[6]Roland H. Bainton, *Here I Stand: A Life of Martin Luther* (New York: Abingdon-Cokesbury, 1950), p. 45.

and that not of yourselves: it is the gift of God: Not of works, lest any man should boast" (Ephesians 2:8-9).

Literally every moment of every day was given to the imitation of some Roman Catholic saint. I was deeply impressed by the lives and deeds of men and women recognized by the various popes as extraordinary individuals. They were patterns for my life. There was a saint for every occasion and need—a pantheon of demigods—enough to satisfy all the contradictory currents of the world. It never occurred to me that it wasn't God, but men and women—the alleged "saints"—that I worshipped. I did not know that some "saints" are nothing more than church resurrections of pagan gods that can be traced back as far as Babylon.

In fact, my goal was to be a saint someday, the real kind, the canonized kind. It wasn't an ego trip but a low-key, intense devotion, wherein suffering was glorified, sometimes coveted. Hence I meticulously recorded even the slightest infraction of the rules, whether in thought, action, or inattention, so that nothing might be overlooked. Then on my knees before the entire religious community in the refectory at mealtime, or alone before the novice master, I acknowledged my unworthiness and my shortcomings.

The Carmelites had two years of novitiate. Many orders require only one year. Sleep, or lack of it, was one of the greatest challenges; I got up at midnight to join with my brothers in chanting fixed prayers and singing Latin canticles for an hour and a quarter. Then we kissed the scapular again and went back to bed, thus assured of salvation for that night, while our superiors felt reassured that no unrighteous or unvirginal thoughts would assail us.

At 5:00 a.m., when sleep was deep, there was an even greater challenge as one of the novices went from floor to floor sounding a loud wooden clapper and shouting, "Praised be Jesus Christ and His Virgin Mother. Arise, Brothers, to pray and praise the Lord."

I always jumped out of bed. We were taught to picture our bed on fire. Thirty minutes later we were all bright and shining for mental prayer. We recited the Divine Office, a formal series of prayers. This was followed by the sacrifice of the mass. By eight or eight-thirty we were poring over the writings of the renowned mystics of Romanism as well as studies in Latin, liturgy, and Gregorian music.

Three evenings a week, the entire Carmelite community gathered in one of the large dark corridors to chant Psalm 51 (50 in the Catholic Bible): *Miserere mei, Deus* ("Have mercy on me, O God"). All the time while reciting this penitential psalm, we flagellated our bare bottoms with a short leather whip. Such activity was to remind us of the implacable and indomitable enemy, the depraved heart.

It was a sign of great spirituality if one performed various kinds of mortification. Lying on the floor at the entrance to the refectory with the monks stepping over you, or kissing the feet of the monks during meal time was to promote poorness of spirit. Carrying a large wooden cross while wearing a crown of thorns, or going from monk to monk to receive the "alapa," or slap on the face, served to deepen an appreciation for the passion of our blessed Lord.

Like most Carmelites, I participated in all these penances. But I honestly preferred some of the other less obvious mortifications, such as wearing the hair shirt (comparable to a cummerbund), which was worn next to the skin, tormenting and scratching the wearer with every move. But worse than the hair shirt was the practice of binding a piece of wire netting around the calf of the leg for several hours. This penance required special permission and later was discouraged because of the danger of cutting off blood circulation and causing blood poisoning. Some Carmelites went without socks in the winter cold. Others allowed pebbles to get into their sandals and remain, so as to endure the discomfort for the Lord. Denying the senses was demanded, especially when it came to looking at women.

An endless list of rules and regulations, running to several volumes, governed the men in sandals. There was "fasting" about six months of the year, when we ate two partial meals and only one full meal for the day. How we looked forward to big holy days, such as the Immaculate Conception of Mary, celebrated December 8th, when there was no fasting.

These acts of asceticism were meant to be lifelong practices. We were taught that self-denial and pain would purify the soul. We prayed that by the mercy of God, through fidelity to His church and its demands that our flesh be mortified, we would have our debts paid and our sins remitted. Thus we would be entitled to a superabundance of merit from the Church of Rome. In that way we would reach a degree of holiness that would deserve a rich reward in Heaven! The more penance we did, the more assured we were that we were reaching consummate perfection, the ultimate spirituality. The prize was far off. It would be realized only after death.

Looking back, I see it all now. Judging by the things we were taught and by the asceticism we practiced, God was in debt to us. He had no choice but to open Heaven's gates to us! We earned it all, but if we failed in some small way, the church had a great repository of merit available through the pope. And, then, the Virgin could help; and in the last analysis even Jesus might be of some help. Today I can hardly help laughing at such ridiculous pretenses. But it is far more sad than humorous.

If the Bible had been a part of our curriculum, we would have known that Jesus dealt with these very same practices and with self-righteousness when He upbraided the Pharisees, whom He called "vipers" (Matthew 12:34). The Pharisees denied themselves many things and made long prayers, but Paul said, "Such practices have indeed the outward appearance of wisdom . . . ; they are of no value . . . but serve only to indulge the old sin nature" (Colossians 2:23, literal Greek). I did not know that the Scriptures say that "all our righteousnesses are as filthy rags" (Isaiah 64:6). How little we understood that through His grace and mercy alone we receive forgiveness of all our sins and receive the Holy Spirit, the Comforter, to live within our hearts and guide us if we will be yielded to Him. As it is written, "Not by works of righteousness which we have done, but according to his mercy he saved us, by the washing of regeneration, and renewing of the Holy Ghost" (Titus 3:5).

Had I known and acknowledged these truths, I would

have been labeled a heretic. As simple as it is, the Word of God is treated as heresy by Rome when it conflicts with church dogma. The Church of Rome can ill afford to acknowledge the truth, for if it did, it would have to rearrange its ways, and it would lose much of the earthly power it gets from its false teaching that priests and the pope are God's dispensers of salvation.

Yet in my ignorance I viewed my first probationary year as one of religious bliss. I was now ready to take the vows of personal poverty, chastity, and obedience. At the beginning of the ceremony we were asked, "What do you seek?" Being young, strong, and idealistic, we gave the answer we had all memorized: "We ask for three things: the mercy of God, the poverty of the order, and the companionship of our brothers." This was our commitment to serve God and His Mother. Completely covered in the brown habits, we prostrated ourselves on the floor. Then the *Te Deum* ("To You, God") was sung and flower petals were strewn over us as we whispered, *"Salve Regina, Mater misericordiae"* ("Hail Holy Queen, Mother of mercy"). By this ceremony we signified our death to the world. We had made our vows to God and Blessed Mary. In the ceremony I had besought her, for I had been taught that without her help I would not be able to save one soul, not even my own.

I have been told that taking these vows is a traumatic experience for some. It wasn't for me. Material possessions meant little in my family. Poverty was no threat! The vow of chastity might have seemed a horrendous undertaking to some, but for me it was nothing. I had never experienced any of the attractions of the world. I wondered how anyone who wanted to be a priest could even allow himself to have unchaste thoughts. Perhaps the most difficult of the three vows was of obedience. At home, however, I had never disregarded my mother's requests or showed indifference to her authority. Therefore, obeying the rector's slightest wish while I was in the seminary came naturally. I would have been willing to water a broomstick, had I been told to do so. Rote obedience was easy, but along with it went an attitude of heart in which things that would have been repulsive, inconvenient, illogical, or even foolish to some were done with gladness. My obedience was made complete, so that I would never think of questioning my superiors or the church. I was to accept what I was told; it was mine to do and die and never to question why.

Some postulants never took their vows; some left the monastery. I was fortunate because neither distress of soul nor despair plagued me. There was only a growing sense of satisfaction in my heart that I was now officially a part of that great order, so rich in history and tradition whose sons and daughters had spilt their blood in furthering the gospel of Rome!

Now I was an integral part of the order, a powerful, spiritual, intellectual, and militant army, whose members would gladly die to promote Rome's authority and control over men and even nations. Even though we might retreat on some point, the retreat would be only temporary, for some strategic or political reason. In the end, Rome would always be victorious.

4 To Be or Not to Be

The two years of probation and arduous study at Brookline ended with both joy and sorrow. I rejoiced in each small new liberty granted us as the strict regimentation was eased. Who would miss the submissiveness? the prolonged silences? the calls at midnight to arise and chant unharmonious Gregorian hymns? Nor would we miss kissing the refectory floor before the community of monks and whispering, *"Mea Culpa"* ("my fault").

We were growing up.

Yet there would be times when we missed the "holiness" of the place, for in that rarefied atmosphere of dedication and devotion, God oftentimes seemed near: we seemed to see Christ in the novice master, the father prior, and the novices. We saw Him in the beauty of nature that surrounded the monastery at 514 Warren Road. We believed we saw Him in the revered relics, in the graven images of saints, in the sacraments, in the adoration of Mary, and especially in the Holy Eucharist.

For six years we had been gestated in the womb of the mother church, bound by increasingly solemn vows, forever tied to her by the umbilical cord of obedience, celibacy, and total dependence for both our physical and spiritual needs. Whatever was required the church provided. This may sound like a wonderful arrangement, but it has its penalties. Many priests, brothers, monks, and nuns, prohibited from a normal life of love, marriage, and children, suffer terrible frustrations. The percentage of those in religious orders who suffer severe emotional distresses or nervous breakdowns is much higher than that of the general population.

Now, after the years of monastic life, our young Catholic minds had been conditioned to respond like Pavlov's dog. We saw what we were trained to see, we heard what we were trained to hear, and we said what we were trained to say. We would go wherever we were told to go and do whatever we were told to do. Anything else was disobedience to the church and, therefore, to God. It was unthinkable!

In this environment, where everything that is taught is guaranteed against error, there was one thing I did not understand. We were told that the next three years at Holy Hill would be devoted chiefly to the study of philosophy. We were warned that philosophical studies might make us apathetic to the disciplines of religious life; so we were urged to apply ourselves in prayer, to practice virtue, and to love obedience. Above all, we must never falter in our unflinching faith and devotion to the one true church.

Somehow the warnings bothered me. Why were they necessary? I found myself wondering why we should study any subject that might cause mischief to our faith. I wanted to know what there was in philosophy that might make me indifferent to religious life; I wanted to avoid anything that might contaminate my faith and fervor.

I hesitated to reveal the full depths of my concern to my superiors. There were three reasons: first, it was almost impossible for me to put my fears into words; second, I could not and would not sin by objecting or by questioning my superiors; and third, I did not want to be "black balled" and possibly dismissed later on. I was sure that I had been called to be God's priest, and I was determined not to allow anything to interfere with my reaching that goal.

I prayed, but my worries persisted. I began to look into the cold and abstract world of philosophy. What I got from my initial studies seemed no more than a survey of mental contortionists who wrestled with themselves. We read John Locke, the English philosopher who taught that all knowledge comes through our five senses and that, therefore, the revelation of God and faith cannot exist. To me that was foolishness; I knew that in every man there is something that yearns to know his origin, his past, and his eternal future—a deep longing that cannot be satisfied by mere sensory perception. Later, when I made cautious inquiries about what our schooling would be, I was told that philosophy, logic, criteriology, metaphysics, and rational psychology would enable us to put those "damnable Protestants" to rout. Good! That inspired me! I was all for that!

I eagerly looked forward to the study of theology, the knowledge of God and His relationships with man and the universe. But theology was scheduled to be last in our training program. In my heart I wondered, "Why?" Why were they leaving this discipline to our final years? I was anxious to know more about the Bible and its teachings.

When I returned to Holy Hill in 1947 after two years at Brookline, I saw why the chamber of commerce listed it as a "must" for all tourists. The rolling hills, the clean, neat barns that dotted the countryside, the clean air, and the sparkling lakes near and far all made me temporarily forget about the dreaded philosophy courses that were required for all those wishing to become priests.

All the major philosophy textbooks were in Latin. No wonder some of us had to study so hard and cram at the last minute for exams! I had a morbid fear of examination time, which was justly called *Dies Irae* ("Day of Wrath"). I was so intent on excelling that I obtained special permission to get up at 3:00 a.m. to prepare for oral and written examinations. In those days the most decisive sign that a student had a calling to the priesthood came when the fathers assembled four times a year to vote on each student priest. As the name of each candidate was brought before the assembly, each priest would cast his vote in a deep wooden jar: a white ball for those considered fit for the priesthood, and a black ball for those to be dismissed. I couldn't think of anything worse than dismissal, a living death. I tried to comfort myself with words that I had heard from somewhere in the Bible: "No man putting his hand to the plough, and looking back, is fit for the kingdom of God" (Luke 9:62, Douay).

Our progress was now measured by our self-imposed discipline; our dedication, obedience, and attitudes; and our skill in scholastic reasoning. We were taught that if we were to win converts to the "one true church," it would be by reasoning. If, for example, we were asked, "Shall a man live again after death?" we were to answer with logic that harmonized with our faith. The Baltimore Catechism and stories of the lives and reappearances of Catholic saints were very important bases for the reasoning and deductive logic needed to answer such a question.

I did not then, and I do not now, have the answers through reasoning, but I do know that philosophy is a finely developed art of reasoning, a tool by which beliefs can be molded or mended. Sometimes it brings truth to light. Just as often it numbs the truth. Friedrich Nietzsche, the German philosopher whose teachings had such enormous influence on Hitler and his belief in a superrace of men and women, is a prime example. In a clever person's hands philosophy can lead to almost any conclusion. And it has! Philosophy has been used by such men as St. Thomas Aquinas to promote false teachings and to elevate pagan traditions and rites to equality with holy Scripture.

Voltaire, the famous French philosopher of the eighteenth century, was considered a great and wise man, but his teachings caused many men and women to despair. He declared, "If [God] cannot prevent evil, He is not almighty; if He will not, He is cruel."[7] He thought that mankind is trivial and unimportant to God. In one of his poems he cried,

Silence! the book of fate is closed to us.
Man is a stranger, devoured by death,
A mockery of fate.
This world, this theater of pride and wrong
Swarms with sick fools who talk of happiness.[8]

---

[7]"The Atheist and the Sage," Ch. IX, in *The Writings of Voltaire* (New York: Wise, 1931), II, p. 175.

[8]Quoted by Will Durant, *The Story of Philosophy* (New York: Simon & Schuster, 1953), p. 172.

So, I observed, as often as not, philosophers are not on speaking terms with simple human wisdom, love, and faith. Today some philosophers and theologians teach doctrines that make revelation and hope fly out the window.

I recall Mother telling me of a conversation she had with Monsignor Cartwright, our pastor at the Cathedral of Saints Peter and Paul in Philadelphia. She had been reading the Bible, despite admonitions not to do so; one day she said to him, "Father, I have been reading the Bible, and as I read, I find real conflicts between the Scriptures and my church that I love."

Monsignor Cartwright replied, "Catherine, we have problems in that regard, but remember what the Bible says about His church: 'The gates of hell shall not prevail against it' [Matthew 16:18]."

This comforted her at the time, but she never forgot the conversation because it showed uncertainty about church doctrine. As she commented to me later, "If, after centuries, the church is still unable to reconcile differences between the Bible and church traditions, something is wrong. There can be no question about it. Where the Bible teaches one thing and the church another, I will choose the Word of God!"

I knew that my mother read the Bible, although I did not fully approve of it. Pope Leo XIII (1878-1903) warned against anyone's getting personal interpretations from Scripture. I thought it better, therefore, to treat the Bible as a closed book insofar as applications to daily life were concerned. I read to Mother the warning against private interpretation of Scripture as contained in the "Encyclical on the Study of Holy Scripture," in the front of the Douay Catholic Bible (1935) under Section V, "The Interpretation of Scripture":

That truth should be sought there where God has placed His treasures, and that the Scriptures are explained without any danger by those with whom is the apostolic succession, was already taught by St. Irenaeus [A.D. 140-202]. It is his doctrine and that of the other Fathers which the Vatican Council adopted when it renewed the decree of the Council of Trent on the interpretation of the written Divine Word, declaring this to be the mind of that council, that in matters of faith and morals, belonging to the building up of Christian doctrine, that is to be regarded as the true sense of Sacred Scripture, which Holy Mother Church has held and holds, to whom it belongs to judge of the true sense and interpretation of the Sacred Scriptures; and that therefore for none was it lawful to interpret Sacred Scripture contrary to the sense, or again contrary to the unanimous consent of the Fathers.

Stripped of its mystical jargon and verbosity, the passage simply means that Catholics are forbidden to accept anything they read in the Bible that is not in strict accord with Catholic teaching. Why? For what reason does the Roman hierarchy seek to make the Bible obscure and unintelligible? Are the Bible's readers so ignorant?

If Catholics are not capable of understanding the Bible, how can they be capable of understanding the writings of "holy fathers"? Did God fail to give biblical authors the ability to write clearly? Of course not. It becomes obvious, then, that the Catholic church does not want its members to find out how false it is and how far it has departed from the Word of God. It wants Catholics to look first to the church, and second, or not at all, to the Bible.

But in seminary days I knew very little about the Scriptures. I longed for America to become Catholic. I thought religious freedom to be a terrible mistake that leads Protestant souls to eternal damnation. My loyalty was to Rome above all else, whether in faith, education, morals, or politics. I was convinced that the Catholic church held the keys to Heaven and was the way to salvation. I was also convinced that if the Catholic clergy and laity were completely indoctrinated and persistent enough, we would eventually make America a Catholic nation. We would bring the Protestants under submission to Rome!

At Holy Hill and, later, at the Discalced Carmelite House of Studies in Washington, D.C., I expected to be invested with the whole armor of Catholic faith and knowledge, so that I could become a warrior priest for His church. I prayed that God would guide me into all truth.

5 The Theology of Rome

The Discalced Carmelite Fathers have a house of studies on Lincoln Road in Washington, D.C., near the Catholic University of America. It was there that I was sent from Holy Hill for a four-year course in theology—the last hurdle on the path to ordination.

I had the idea that theology would be easier than philosophy. A lot of us did. But the intricacies of the one were not less than those of the other. Nevertheless, I found theology far more interesting and "spiritual" than philosophy.

From early childhood I had looked upon each priest as another Christ, Heaven's emissary, able to expound and explain God's holy Word. I felt sure that the learned priests and teachers at Lincoln Road would remove the clouds of ignorance from my eyes. Mysteries would be unfolded, and at my teachers' blessed feet I would feed on the manna of God's Word and learn His sacred laws as revealed in the Bible. I would learn their application to life, for I was determined to be perfect through the grace of Jesus Christ. Yet I knew in my own heart that it is impossible for anyone to keep the whole Law. Over and over I pondered the words, "For whosoever shall keep the whole law, and yet offend in one point, he is guilty of all" (James 2:10).

What should I do, then, that I might keep from sin and appear blameless before God?

I believed that by living in the sterile atmosphere of the monastery or in a priesthood separated from the world, I would not be contaminated. Or perhaps I might be martyred—tortured and murdered for the church—and in such an event my great and noble deeds would win eternal glory. I renounced my worldly desires and loved poverty, considering the modern world and all its allurements to be snares and delusions. I would try to keep the Law.

I did not know the glorious words of the Apostle Paul, "For by grace are ye saved through faith; and that not of yourselves: it is the gift of God: Not of works, lest any man should boast" (Ephesians 2:8-9). Nor did I know the certainty of salvation to them that believe on His name, for as the Apostle wrote in his letter to the Romans, "I am persuaded that neither death, nor life, nor angels, nor principalities, nor powers, nor things present, nor things to come, Nor height, nor depth, nor any other creature, shall be able to separate us from the love of God, which is in Christ Jesus our Lord" (Romans 8:38-39).

Instead of studying the whole volume of the Bible, we studied church decrees, canon law, and the writings of church fathers. This brought up some difficult questions. For example, Canon V On Baptism reads, "If anyone saith, that baptism is free, that is, not necessary unto salvation; let him be anathema [accursed]."[9] So we moralized on its meaning. What happens when there is no water available for baptism? Suppose a lost soul were converted to Catholicism on his deathbed; could he be baptized with something other than water, such as milk, wine, or saliva? Would the unbaptized soul go to eternal Hell for want of a little water to baptize him? Or what about the wounded soldier in a foxhole or a sailor facing certain death on a sinking ship? If he cries out with his dying breath, "Lord, have mercy on me; forgive me my sins," but cannot be baptized, is he doomed to Hell's eternal fires?

---

[9] *The Canons and Decrees of the Sacred and Ecumenical Council of Trent,* trans. J. Waterworth (Chicago: Christian Symbolic Publication Society, [1848]), p. 82.

It is unfortunate that we did not look to the Bible for answers. When Jesus was dying on the cross between two thieves, one "said unto Jesus, Lord, remember me when thou comest into thy kingdom. And Jesus said unto him, Verily I say unto thee, To day shalt thou be with me in paradise" (Luke 23:42-43). Baptism cannot be necessary for salvation.

What about a baby that dies without baptism? Is it lost? The Gospel of Matthew records that Jesus called a little child unto Him and said, "Whosoever therefore shall humble himself as this little child, the same is the greatest in the kingdom of heaven. And whoso shall receive one such little child in my name receiveth me" (Matthew 18:4-5). God is just! The Bible says, "Great and marvelous are thy works, Lord God Almighty; just and true are thy ways" (Revelation 15:3). Babies return to God's loving care.

Over and over, the Bible makes it clear that the blood of Christ, and nothing else, is the cleansing agent for man's sins. Water baptism saves no one any more than walking into a church and attending a service assures one of salvation. It is receiving Christ that counts.

We also spent many days discussing two types of sin, venial sins (little sins) and mortal sins. No one has ever defined exactly what venial sins are, but they are said to be too minor to bar one from communion. If unconfessed, however, they might add to the amount of time one spends in purgatory after death. For example, "white lies" are not considered to be anything more than venial sins, especially if, when telling the lie, one makes a mental reservation for purposes of evasion. He can simply say to himself, "I didn't really mean it." Even if one is sworn in court to tell the truth, he need not do so if he is sure he cannot be caught or thinks he might be damaged by telling the whole truth.

We discussed stealing and cursing. Are such acts sins? We learned that it is only a venial sin for a servant to steal small amounts from his employer, and it is only a venial sin to steal to give to the church. One may curse another's personal possessions, but it is a mortal sin to curse a person.

Mortal sin bars one from communion and, if unconfessed, puts the sinner in danger of Hell's fire. The list of mortal sins is almost endless, including such things as entering into a second marriage while the first spouse is living; rejecting the articles of faith, such as those published by the Council of Trent; denying the bodily assumption of the Virgin Mary into Heaven; denying papal infallibility; or willfully missing mass more than one week. Adultery is a mortal sin, but if the adulterer or adulteress confesses and is forgiven, he or she may thereafter deny the act; once forgiven, it is cancelled as if it never happened.

Innocent III (1198-1216) declared that "the faithful must confess their sins to a priest at least once a year under pain of mortal sin."

The handling of sin by the Catholic church is something like transactions at the bank. When a person sins, he thereby overdraws his account of God's love and mercy. The amount of his overdraft depends on how serious the sin is. He may go to confession and obtain from the priest at least partial forgiveness—which is, of course, a resupply of God's mercy. The supply never runs out, especially if the sinner appeals to Mary, who is a special source of merit and grace for sinners; St. Anselm (1033-1109) even said, "At times we are saved more quickly by invoking Mary's name than by invoking the name of Jesus."[10] Catholic doctrine declares that Christ listens to Mary because she is the Mother of God. Therefore, she is called upon to be the intercessor between God and man. This is set forth in the rosary, which contains fifty "Hail Marys":

Hail Mary, full of grace, the Lord is with thee; blessed art thou among women, and blessed is the fruit of thy womb, Jesus. Holy Mary, Mother of God, pray for us sinners now, and at the hour of our death. Amen.

The tradition of worshipping the Queen of Heaven is of pagan origin; such false religion is denounced in Jeremiah 44:25. Not even one verse in the entire Bible calls Mary the

---

[10]Quoted by St. Alphonsus Maria de Ligouri, *The Glories of Mary* (Baltimore: Helicon, 1962), I, p. 164.

Queen of Heaven. The Virgin Mary herself sang, "My soul doth magnify the Lord, And my spirit hath rejoiced in God my Saviour" (Luke 1:46-47). Although she was indeed "blessed" among women, Mary needed a Saviour too, just as anyone else does. She is not an intercessor, for only Christ is the Intercessor between God and men (I Timothy 2:5). Only God can forgive sin. The Bible tells us, "Let us therefore come boldly unto the throne of grace, that we may obtain mercy, and find grace to help in time of need" (Hebrews 4:16). Nothing needs to be added or taken away. "He is the propitiation for our sins: and not for our's only, but also for the sins of the whole world" (I John 2:2).

People love authority in a disordered world. Many seek a sign, a person, an image, a cathedral, rich vestments, and a holy mien that they can see and touch. Yet no matter how beautiful or holy these things may appear, they are worthless adornments insofar as our salvation is concerned. As the Bible says, "The just shall live by his faith."

Our studies in theology were often exercises in fear. So much was said about the awesome power of the pope and his church that we dared not offend by questioning our superiors too closely about the decrees and dogma of the church; for there are literally hundreds of "anathemas" against those who reject or condemn any of the Catholic church's claims, no matter how absurd. (To be "anathema" means to be cursed, damned, excommunicated, and consigned to Hell.)

The awesome powers of the pope were further impressed on us by the doctrines of papal infallibility. When the pope speaks *ex cathedra*—in his official capacity as head of the church—he is said to be "possessed of that infallibility with which the Divine Redeemer . . . willed that his Church should be endowed for defining doctrine regarding faith or morals."[11] In 1870, during Vatican I, Pope Pius IX proclaimed, "I am the way and the truth, and the life; no man cometh unto the Father but by me." The crowd roared, *"Viva Pio Nono [IX], Papa infallible!"("long live Pius IX, infallible pope!").* It was reported that while Pope Pius spoke, a terrible

---

[11]Vatican I, quoted by Rahner, p. 229.

storm and a dense darkness descended over the city of Rome, and water, pouring through broken glass in the roof, splashed close to the pope. Some compared the event to Moses' receiving of the Law on Mount Sinai, but many saw the storm as a sign of God's wrath.

We were taught some incredible things about the Host, the wafer that Catholics receive in communion. Canon I On the Most Holy Sacrament of the Eucharist reads, "If anyone denieth, that, in the sacrament of the most holy Eucharist, are contained truly, really, and substantially, the body and blood together with the soul and divinity of our Lord Jesus Christ, and consequently the whole Christ; but saith that He is only therein as in a sign, or in figure, or virtue; let him be anathema."[12] In other words, we were taught that when the priest hovers over the wafer and says, "This is my body," it becomes the actual flesh of Christ. Likewise, after the priest says the words, "This is my blood," the wine is said to become the actual blood of Jesus. It is true that Jesus said, "This is my body ... this is my blood," but it is obvious that He was speaking figuratively, just as He did when He said, "I am the true vine, and my Father is the husbandman" (John 15:1).

This dogma about the Host—sometimes called the "wafer-God"—has given rise to some strange doings. If, for example, the consecrated Host is dropped and a mouse or other animal snatches the wafer away, the priest is given a forty-day penance to perform. If the sacramental wine is spilt at the mass, the priest is advised to lick it up and clean the place with a special cloth called a purificator. If the priest vomits after consuming the bread or the wine, it is recommended that he consume the vomit, provided that he can do it without creating an embarrassing scene. The alternative is to burn what he vomited. And such things have happened many times; I myself recall times that mass was being said on tossing Navy ships and the priest became seasick.

Charles H. Spurgeon, the great English preacher of the nineteenth century, said that "the worship of what is called the Blessed Sacrament is as vile an idolatry as the worship by

---

[12] *Dogmatic Canons and Decrees* (Rockford, Ill.: Tan Books), p. 82.

the Egyptians of onions and other pot-herbs which grew in their own gardens."[13]

Today in several American convents where the wafer is prepared and baked, a wafer is placed on a monstrance—a gold or silver vessel—and kept on the altar for all to see. Twenty-four hours a day, every day, nuns take turns kneeling before the altar in perpetual adoration of the Host.

In 1952, I was twenty-seven and in my second year of theology when I received three major orders; one of these ordained me as a subdeacon, an order that has been discontinued since Vatican II. This order permitted me to bless objects, so I blessed everything I saw in Washington, D.C.: the Washington Monument, Lincoln's Memorial, and hundreds of other places. I could also officially wear the Roman collar. I went for long walks around the city with other Carmelites so that I could show off "the collar." Few things brought such personal satisfaction, for I could read the obeisance and reverence in the eyes of many Catholic passersby.

During the last year before ordination, I set up an improvised altar in my cell in order to practice the celebration of the mass. It was more complicated than it is now, but for me, the honor of changing bread and wine into the "glorified" flesh and blood of Christ was so great that I resolved to offer a flawless mass. I was determined to master all the rubrics and ceremonies "in order to celebrate it as Christ did at the Last Supper." Every day for a year I went through the motions of this pageant. As priest-celebrant, I reenacted the experiences of Christ from the supper in the upper room through His agony in the garden, His betrayal, His trial and crucifixion, and His death, burial, and resurrection. It is a drama crowding the details of many days into the space of one hour or less.

The mass involved making the sign of the cross sixteen times, lifting the eyes to heaven eleven times, kissing the altar eight times, folding the hands four times, striking the breast

---

[13]"On Whose Side Are You?" *The Metropolitan Tabernacle Pulpit* (Pasadena, Texas: Pilgrim, 1972), XXVI, p. 214.

ten times, bowing the head twenty-one times, genuflecting eight times, bowing the shoulders seven times, blessing the altar with the sign of the cross thirty times, laying the hands flat on the altar twenty-nine times, praying secretly eleven times, praying aloud thirteen times, taking the bread and wine and changing it into the body and blood of Christ, covering and uncovering the chalice ten times, and going to and fro twenty times. I cite this to show the ritualistic detail it encompassed.

Since Vatican II, the mass has undergone considerable simplification, but back then, one had to master all the Latin and the various intonations and do it all gracefully. It demanded literally hundreds of hours of practice. I went through so many "dry" masses that when it was time for the real thing, I had mastered the motions perfectly and was able to project an atmosphere of holiness and worship. This was glorious! I was God's priest! And I had the pope's word for it as decreed by the Council of Trent!

As the day of ordination came closer, I dreaded some accident, such as a car wreck, preventing my ordination. It was too good to be true that soon I would be a priest. The eleven long years of repeating daily the words, "I wish, I can, I will!" were coming to an end. Nothing mattered any more except the priesthood—not my family, my friends, or anything else! I had been prepared. I was ready!

Dr. Brewer began wearing the Roman collar while studying in the seminary in Washington, D.C. "I went for long walks around the city with other Carmelites so that I could show off 'the collar.'"

6 I Am Ordained

June 6, 1953, was the day I had waited for—the day of my ordination at the Shrine of the Immaculate Conception of Mary in Washington, D.C.

My heart was filled with inexpressible joy and gratitude that the impossible dream was about to be realized. I would be a priest "after the order of Melchisedec," a "priest of the most high God." At my bidding during my celebration of the mass, Christ Himself would come down. Through the transubstantiation of the bread and wine, His flesh and blood would become my possessions. At that moment, I would be equal with Him, elevated above the angels, performing functions holier than any other.

On that glorious morning, more than twenty of us ordinands arrived at the shrine. There were Dominicans, Augustinians, Franciscans, Capuchins, Paulists, Trinitarians, Josephites, and Oblates of Mary. I happened to be the only Discalced Carmelite. Vested in robes as deacons, we moved in solemn procession through the large crowd gathered for the occasion. In that crowd were friends and relatives, but more precious to me than all other visitors were my own mother and brother. His Excellency, Bishop McNamara, began the mass; then the archdeacon called us forward, and we knelt in a semicircle before the bishop.

We were warned by the archdeacon that no one was to come forward for ordination under false pretext. The bishop then charged that our personal lives were to be exemplary and pleasing to God, that by both preaching and example we would build the house of God. We were told, "The Priest is ordained to offer Sacrifice, to bless, to guide, to preach, and to baptize. With great awe, then, should one advance to so high a state."[14]

As we then prostrated ourselves on the floor where we had been kneeling, the Litany of the Saints was sung; afterwards, we knelt again in silence before the bishop, and he, followed by the priests, laid both hands on our heads. The bishop and the priests kept their right hands extended over us while the bishop recited the prayer of ordination.

Next our hands were bound with a white cloth and consecrated. This ceremony symbolized the fact that as priests we would bless and consecrate sacred objects in the name of Christ, but even more than that, we would hold in our mortal hands the Host, which we believed would become the literal body and blood of our Lord. At that time we were given the power to offer sacrifice to God by celebrating masses for both the living and the dead. From this moment we were officially ordained Roman Catholic priests. We then joined the bishop in the concelebration of the mass.

When the ceremony was completed, the bishop gave a final address, reminding us to consider attentively the order we had taken and to remember from this time onward that as priests, "in the highest rank of Holy Order we must try to live up to the example of Jesus Christ who was truly God and truly man, and remember that at the sacrifice of the mass, we would be made one with Christ, Himself, offering once again his body and his blood for our redemption." We were reminded again that in the confessional we would be as one with God, having from God the power to forgive sins. Even in our ordinary lives, we would be as the Son of Man, calling ourselves as the pope, *"Servus servorum Dei"* ("Servant of the servants of God"). We were then instructed that after our first mass we should say three other masses: one of the Holy Ghost, a second of the blessed Mary, "ever virgin," and a

---

[14] *The Ordination of a Priest* (Paterson, N.J.: St. Anthony Guild Press, 1940), p. 10.

third for the faithful departed. The ceremony was completed with the reading of John 1.

At last, a priest! Outside the vast shrine my mother and brother, classmates, friends, and relatives knelt on the ground to kiss the palms of the hands which, moments before, had been anointed with holy oil and consecrated to tell the whole world of its indelible bond to Christ. That kiss, according to the church, earns them an indulgence of one hundred days.

Many years have passed since that memorable day, and much happiness and sorrow have marked my pathway. But I have never forgotten the quiet and solemn contemplation of God that came over me as I realized that I had been invested with sacerdotal powers to dispense the means of salvation. A deep inner satisfaction filled me as I thought of the words of the famous French orator priest, Lacordaire: "To live in the midst of the world with no desires for its pleasures; to be a member of every family, yet belong to none; to share all sufferings; to penetrate all secrets; to heal all wounds; to go daily from men to God; to offer him as their homage and petitions; to return to God from men and then bring his pardon and his hope; to have a heart of bronze for chastity; to teach and instruct; to pardon and console; to bless and to be blessed forever! O God! What a life, and 'tis thine, O priest of Jesus Christ!" The words were beautiful, almost hypnotic, to me.

My first mass the next morning at the Carmelite Chapel on Lincoln Road was a highlight of my life to that time. With my brother Paul serving the mass, I undertook to be perfect in every detail. I wanted the ceremony to have an aura of holiness and grace. Having the mass was having God, and having the church was having Heaven. The mass was Christ, and Christ was the mass. The thought that I could bring Him from Heaven to earth every day for the remaining days of my life, by pronouncing a few words, made me intoxicated with the joys of thanksgiving. That I could handle Him so freely and give Him to others made me proud that I had such authority and power in God's church. I was at the zenith of all I had wished for, and I intended to exercise it for the good of every Catholic and everyone I could win to the "mother church."

It is traditional for the new priest to go to his home parish to sing his first Solemn High Mass. That meant going to the Cathedral of Saints Peter and Paul in Philadelphia. Hundreds of invitations went out for this gala event and the banquet that followed. Friends, relatives, priests, and nuns were present. Monsignor Cartwright, the rector of the cathedral and one who had greatly encouraged me to be a priest, assisted me as archdeacon. Two Carmelite priests who were my personal friends also assisted me. A very close Carmelite friend of mine through seminary and monastery years, Father William McNamara, delivered the message. His theme was "Enthusiasm," and he spoke of the enthusiasm that I had displayed all through the years of preparation for the priesthood.

As the mass got underway, I was captivated by its beauty, majesty, and glory. As a little boy, I had heard men like Father Gallagher and Father McVeigh sing out, but now it was I. It was almost unreal to hear my own voice reaching out among the pillars and arches of the huge cathedral. Someone said that as I sang the Gloria and the Credo, parts of the mass, I appeared as transfixed. After all, I was continuing the sacrifice of Christ's death. It is said that even an angel cannot say mass. I believed that I was giving God to mankind in the Eucharist. I believed that I was holding the place of God!

After a few weeks of vacation I returned to Washington, D.C., for my last year of theology. I worked hard, but I was no longer frightened, because I knew that I was a priest and that no one, nothing, could take that away from me, not even if I failed oral and written examinations. I did well, however, and received permission to preach and to hear confession.

Now, I was a priest.

7 Celibacy and Confessions

It was a boiling hot afternoon in Washington, D.C., when I was urgently summoned to the chapel to hear my first confession. I had no idea who it was. I wasn't supposed to know, but I couldn't help wondering. Would it be a man? a woman? or a child?

As I headed toward the confessional box, a feeling of apprehension swept over me. This was a real confession! Suddenly I felt uneasy. Something inside me whispered, "By what right do you hear this person's innermost secrets? By what right do you, a mere man and a sinner, forgive sin? How can you take the place of God? How can it be that God does not hear the voice of a repentant sinner without coming to you?"

I hoped that it would be something minor, perhaps the confession of some venial sins, or perhaps an expression of sorrow for sin already confessed, for such is a fairly common occurrence.

Hurrying toward the chapel, I kept telling myself that nothing was going to shock me, no matter how lurid the confession might be. People are human. People sin. They need forgiveness, and it was my duty to hear, to question, and to forgive. So I took courage in the thought that this would be my first of countless opportunities through which I could show forth the mercy and love of Christ to the sinner. "Nothing will shock me! Nothing will shock me!" I kept saying. I recalled the words of one of the retreat masters at Holy Hill, who had quoted St. John of the Cross, a sixteenth-century Carmelite, as saying, "A saint is never scandalized." The retreat master had also quoted St. Augustine's description of the confessional as "the most dangerous duty of a priest." I uttered a prayer, "Lord, I want to be a saint. Let me not be offended by any confession."

Taking my place in the middle section of the confessional box, I had the feeling that I was acting in God's place. I was His mediator. At that moment I felt both pride and humility that the Roman system of apostleship had conferred such powers on me. I, Father Brewer, had become a priest by the laying on of hands.

When I slid back the door covering the opaque screen between the penitent and me, a man's voice on the other side said, "Bless me, Father. It has been two weeks since my last confession. I confess to Almighty God, to the Blessed Virgin Mary, to Blessed Michael the Archangel, to Blessed John the Baptist, to the Holy Apostles Peter and Paul, to all the saints, and to you, Father, that I have sinned exceedingly in thought, word, and deed, through my fault, through my fault, through my most grievous fault." Having thus repeated the first part of the confiteor, the formal prayer for forgiveness, he went on, "I am a Catholic priest, and here are my sins."

My heart jumped, and for an instant I felt as if my head was whirling. My first penitent—a priest! I would have fled but for fear of offending God.

What followed was a lengthy, graphic description of one sexual affair after another. His confession was a detailed account of seductions and conquests in rapid succession. Even during confession, I could not help feeling that he enjoyed describing his affairs. Waves of disbelief assailed me, but I remembered, "A saint is never scandalized!" As he continued, however, he seemed to grow more contrite, and I began to feel compassion for him. I knew that I was supposed to question him on any point that was not clear to me, so that I could determine the full gravity of his sins and thus better judge what penance to assign him. At one point I wanted to ask, "Were any of the women you seduced married women?" I didn't have to ask. He told me that some of them were.

I didn't question him at all. I was confused. I even wondered if this was a "bogus priest" or whether it was some awful joke that was being played on me by the very Devil himself. I wondered if he knew who I was, and I half expected him to laugh at me before it was over.

After what seemed like hours, his confession was done. I gave him penance, and as he requested I granted him forgiveness: "I absolve thee from thy sins in the name of the Father and the Son and the Holy Ghost. Amen."[15]

That first confession clearly urged on me the need for spartan self-discipline. More than ever I was determined to deny my senses. I would do anything to mortify my flesh, die to self, practice mental self-discipline, and walk uprightly before God. I resolved that with God's help such temptations would never overcome me. But later on, in moments unaware, I wondered, is adultery all that easy? I had thought that fornication and adultery were rare sins, but now I realized that they were easy and common. I realized how naive I was. I wanted to forget, but I could not. My naivete and ignorance bothered me, and I began to rationalize.

Washington has thousands of beautiful young secretaries, and I wondered if I was being too self-righteous in my attitudes. What harm could there be in "looking" at the pretty girls? What was wrong with dreaming a little? Didn't God make women too? Wouldn't their beauty remind me of the wonderful works of creation and the mysteries of life? I told myself that the appeal of the fairer sex was nothing more than an appreciation of beauty, and that it would go no farther than that. But something inside whispered that I was lying to myself.

I held to my vow of chastity because my office as priest strictly forbade sexual relationships. Oftentimes I wondered, "What is love? How does one know when he is in love? How can I escape these sensual thoughts? What would I do if I saw some pretty girl and wanted to see her again? Should I run

---

[15]Ludwig Ott, *Fundamentals of Catholic Dogma,* ed. James Canon Bastible, trans. Patrick Lynch (Rockford, Ill.: Tan Books, 1974), p. 436.

away? Am I strong enough to withstand every temptation that might come my way?"

It was, perhaps, because of these reflections on love and life that I undertook a detailed examination of myself. In that cold, rigid atmosphere of the monastery, I had vowed to remain celibate, forever chaste. Now I wondered if I ought to cultivate a disdain for women and avoid them as much as possible. No! That would be an unwise course leading to all kinds of aberrant behavior. Hermits may retire to their caves in order to avoid the world and all its temptations, but they are not, then, victorious over the flesh or the Devil. A victorious person *overcomes* temptation.

Celibacy is not supported by any Scripture. It is against nature. The Apostle Peter was married (Matthew 8:14); so were most of the men and women of the early church. So I pondered the question, "If a celibate falls in love or succumbs to the temptations of the flesh, who is more to blame, the church or the celibate?"

I tried to reason it out by common sense—not by what the church says, but by observations and careful study—and when I saw the answer, it pained me deeply. It was like a man finding out that his mother is a selfish, scheming hypocrite. Rome's purpose is the total control of the labor, money, property, and actions of every Catholic priest, monk, brother, and nun. All the clever arguments in the world will not dispel that simple fact.

A surprising number of such religious devotees become bitterly disillusioned; some even become atheists. Thousands would leave the Catholic church, but they have no place else to go. What can they do? Who will care? Most of them believe that all Protestants are enemies. Some who leave the church are shunned by former friends and treated as a disgrace by Catholic relatives.

The system of celibacy is utterly mischievous and the cause of much immorality and aberrant behavior, including homosexuality. Its abolition is being advocated from within and without the Catholic church, but to no avail. During his visit to Germany in November 1980, Pope John Paul II described priestly celibacy as an "illustrious legacy of the church" and criticized attempts to weaken it.

How fortunate is the suffering one who sees this ridiculous restriction in time and finds an understanding spouse. It is truly said that the religious devotee who leaves the cold, rigid restrictions of Catholicism can find a new life of truth and freedom flowing from the sunlight of God's Word.

Although my first experience in hearing confession had been harsh and disturbing, I soon adjusted, although I never liked the duty. I was an idealist. I had always loved people. I felt compassion toward all as I daily heard their sins and saw their needs. I wanted to help. Because I was quick to forgive and slow to punish, I became known as Father "One Hail Mary Bart."

Canon VI On the Most Holy Sacrament of Penance reads, "If anyone denieth, either that sacramental confession was instituted, or is necessary to salvation, of divine right; or saith, that the manner of confessing secretly to a priest alone, which the Church hath ever observed from the beginning, and doth observe, is alien from the institution and command of Christ, and is a human invention; let him be anathema."[16]

This canon is a classic example of the misuse of Scripture. Confession to a priest, secretly or openly, was not commanded or ordained by Christ. Nowhere does the Bible say that such confession is necessary for salvation. The confessional is a mere invention of men. There is nothing in Scripture to support the sacrament of penance or even purgatory!

It is the privilege of every sinner, whoever he may be, to confess his sins directly to God. This is the meaning of repentance. "He [God] is faithful and just to forgive us our sins, and to cleanse us from all unrighteousness" (I John 1:9). "There is one God, and one mediator between God and men, the man Christ Jesus" (I Timothy 2:5). "We have an advocate with the Father, Jesus Christ the righteous" (I John 2:1). Since only God can forgive sin, it is blasphemy for any man to claim that he can take God's place in absolving man of his sins.

---

[16]*Canons and Decrees,* p. 108.

Why does the church hold to the confessional as such an important part of its dogma? The chief reason is that obligatory confession keeps Catholics in submission. Penitents are taught that confession is one of the most important acts of life, without which one's soul may suffer eternal Hell. A complete confession, with nothing held back, is said to be necessary for peace with God. Many Catholics live in terror of forgetting to confess some sin and consequently suffering longer in purgatory.

I was told of a young woman who found her six-month-old baby girl dead in the crib. The baby's regular feeding time was 6:00 a.m., but the mother overslept one morning and didn't arise until about seven. The doctors told her that the baby's death was completely beyond her control, that it was that strange thing known as "crib death" that happens perhaps once in fifty thousand cases. But she blamed herself. She thought that if she had arisen at the normal time, she might have saved her child's life, and she considered herself guilty of mortal sin.

A few days after the baby's death, the mother was involved in a painful automobile accident. Enroute to the hospital she cried over and over, "Am I going to die? ... Please don't let me die! ... I am damned! ... I haven't been to confession! ... Get me a priest! ... Please! ... Please!"

I was told the woman did not die from her injuries. She was counseled by doctors and others who had had the same experience, and she eventually came to understand that the baby's death was not her fault.

The Bible says, "the gift of God is eternal life" (Romans 6:23). Jesus said, "My sheep hear my voice, and I know them, and they follow me: And I give unto them eternal life; and they shall never perish, neither shall any man pluck them out of my hand. My Father, which gave them me, is greater than all; and no man is able to pluck them out of my Father's hand" (John 10:27-29). The Catholic church ignores this truth, teaching instead that Catholics may be lost or may suffer long torment in purgatory if they commit even one mortal sin that at death remains unconfessed and unforgiven. This bondage exists to this day because it serves the purpose of the church.

The mischief done by the confessional cannot be exaggerated. Even in the Middle Ages, it served as a feeder for a vast intelligence network. When kings, presidents, and generals confess, the Catholic church becomes privy to a nation's most important secrets. To this day, the Vatican's intelligence operations are among the best in the world. There is virtually no nation in the world whose secrets have not been penetrated by the Vatican at one time or another, and in Catholic nations, that penetration is complete.

Most priests are gentle and kind; but if they wish, they can examine every detail and secret of their parishioners. This can have tremendous effects, for knowledge is power. If one knows a person's financial or social position, beliefs, politics, purposes, wrongdoings, and conflicts, he can exert tremendous force. A priest can know more about a man than his wife does. Children often furnish information unwittingly. Sometimes husbands and wives draw apart, fearing that the other has told the priest some secret.

The confessional, linked as it is to penances and purgatory, is a yoke of bondage to Catholics, not only in this life but even beyond the grave, as masses and prayers for the dead are said.

Yet purgatory, prayers for the dead, and secret auricular confession to a priest have no support whatsoever in Scripture. They are not even traditions from the time of Christ, since they were not instituted until at least the fourth century.

Can any priest, then, claim that he has the power to dispense salvation?

8 To the Philippines

Several years before my ordination to the priesthood, I had met Father Patrick Shanley, a missionary to the Philippines. He was an impressive man, especially to me, because of the wonderful stories he told about the people and the many opportunities for service in the Far East. It was thrilling to hear him describe the Philippines and the remarkable diversity of its people, ranging from the cosmopolitan, urbane citizens of Manila to aborigines barely out of the Stone Age and animists worshipping the sun, the moon, trees, flowers, and the wind.

One day when we were talking about the Islands, I asked, "Do you think I might be suitable for missionary service there?" He thought a moment and then said, "Bart, you're just the kind of man we need there." It was like a blessing and an invitation; from that day on I wanted to be a missionary. When the time came for us newly ordained priests to embark on our careers, I asked to be sent to the Philippines.

When my request was approved, I was ecstatic with joy. A new life was before me. I envisioned myself making heroic sacrifices, serving God without limit, free from the restrictions of the monastery. It could mean adventure, maybe even martyrdom on some wild and isolated emerald island. That would be the epitome of sanctity, the threshhold of sainthood. I was ready to be God's man, His servant *usque ad mortem* ("until death").

It wasn't easy saying good-bye to my mother and my brother, for I loved them dearly and knew they loved me too. Yet I felt my path was laid out by God, and I took comfort in Jesus' words, "He that loveth father or mother more than me is not worthy of me" (Matthew 10:37). Surely my assignment to the Philippines was a fulfillment, the reason for my twelve years of study and contemplation in the cloistered halls of Carmelite monasteries.

Eagerly I began to prepare, wanting to know as much as I could about the people living on that cluster of seven thousand islands stretching more than eleven hundred miles north and south in the western Pacific Ocean. I began to acquire a rudimentary knowledge of Tagalog, a language spoken by the people on the largest island, Luzon. More than eighty languages and dialects are spoken in the Philippines. English and Spanish are the languages used in business and government, but Tagalog is spoken more widely than any other native language. Knowledge of it would enable me to go into areas far from the beaten paths of traders and prospectors. I wanted to reach the lost and bring them into the church.

En route to my new post, I was invited to visit the beautiful retreat of the Irish Discalced Carmelite Fathers tucked away in the hills near Redlands, California. There I became acquainted with a seasoned Carmelite missionary priest who was returning to the Islands, and together we sailed from Long Beach, California, on Sunday, October 31, 1954, the Roman Catholic feast day of Christ the King.

As our ship plowed through the blue waters of the Pacific, I thought how wonderful it is to be alive if we go with God in this beautiful world. How wonderful that He Who made the land, the seas, the heavens, the sun, the moon, and the stars has promised to keep watch over us. For as it is written, even a sparrow does not fall without His knowledge (Matthew 10:29).

I could not help being reminded that while the pope of Rome wears a triple crown of gold and jewels, Jesus wore only a crown of thorns. While bishops have their thrones, Jesus warned a man who said he would follow Him, "The foxes have holes, and the birds of the air have nests; but the Son of man hath not where to lay his head" (Matthew 8:20). How could I fail to adore Him? I prayed that the Virgin Mary and the saints would bless and guide me and that I would bring many souls to Catholicism.

Sixteen days after we left Long Beach, we arrived in Manila. Any fears I had in seeing my new home were quickly dispelled when I saw far below the main deck of our ship a small group waving to us from the dock. Six people—three Carmelites, a Dominican priest, and a handsome couple— were waiting to make our arrival a joyous occasion. I was introduced to two wonderful people, Jim and Tina Norton, both devout Catholics and also prominent business people. They helped us through customs and commenced my intro- duction to the Islands. I felt at home as we walked along Ayala Boulevard, where some of the buildings reminded me of New York City. The old walled city, which bore the worst scars of Japan's three years of occupation, was sadly impressive.

The kaleidoscope of colors, the frenzied rush, and the cacophony of sounds were to me a glorious scene of organized confusion. Fringe-topped, gaily painted jeepneys dashed about amidst countless produce carts while open-air marketers hawked everything from papayas to bolts of silk. It was exciting to watch sellers and buyers engaged in some wild, feverish contest, haggling over prices. The gesturing, shouting, and rushing seemed like the inception of a riot. Bare survival seemed a miracle to my wondering eyes; but in the colorful circus of merchandise, people went their way laughing and talking. It was a sight that never grew old to me.

Vestiges of centuries of Spanish influence in the Philippines still linger on. Several million people speak Spanish. Old churches and forts dot the larger islands. Beautiful statues, grilled windows, and central plazas may still be found in Old Manila, and the four-hundred-year-old walled city still boasts the replica of a Spanish town. The old Quiapo Church, near the heart of the city, escaped most of the ravages of war and is still a center of worship. Every day hundreds of candles burn before the image known as "The

Black Nazarene." Long queues of Catholic faithful walk on their knees the length of the church, reciting the rosary, seeking favor with God through the Virgin Mary.

The more I learned about the Filipinos, the more I grew to love them. I found them exceedingly attractive, colorful, talented, musical, and eager to learn. From my first days there I sensed in many of them a simple, childlike faith. They responded to instruction, almost eager to be convinced that we priests were the sole custodians of God's grace and mercy. I perceived, too, that such trust imposed an awesome responsibility on me as a missionary priest. I sought the friendship of all—Roman Catholics, Protestants, even those who claimed allegiance to no god. It became clear that I could reach them best by showing Christlike tenderness, simple compassion, and patience. It was an attitude that did not always win favor with my brother priests. I would pay for this later on.

After a few weeks I was anxious to leave Manila for my new post in the little town of Baler. When the day for departure came, we headed for the airport, because it was not safe to go to Baler by road. Outlying regions of the Islands, including Luzon, were still subject to attacks by the fierce Hukbalahaps, or Huks ("People's Anti-Japanese Army"), a Communist-led guerrilla force numbering more than 150,000. Their raids and destruction of life and property threatened the rural areas and even the central government.

As the Philippine Airlines plane took off for its first stop, I was enraptured by the scenery. We flew past areas where Ifugao tribesmen have labored more than two thousand years, terracing the verdant mountains to a height of more than twenty-five hundred feet above the valley floors. From the air the terraces look like giant green stairways to the sky. To this day I have never seen anything more remarkable than those giant stairs, cultivated by rice farmers and edged with mortarless walls as much as sixty feet high. The steps range in size from that of a bungalow to many acres, making a beauty that can hardly be described. Then we flew over dense forests, thriving coconut plantations, and long, sandy beaches.

When we landed, a jeep took us to the mission

compound. The Mount Carmel High School students were playing basketball when I arrived. When they saw me, several shouted, "We want the new father to play ball with us." With a slight nod from the senior pastor, I took off my habit and joined them. The new padre became an instant success.

It was there that I met a haughty Italian priest who showed a dislike for me from the first, and I soon learned that he was anti-American. He did not like my easy manner of fraternization with people of all ranks and religion; he referred to me several times as a "Protestant priest." At first his churlish manner upset me, and I wondered why he disliked me so. I was acting in accordance with Jesus' teachings; I felt that I had no apologies to make for my methods.

Then I began to understand. Unintentionally I brought him discomfort. He believed in stern authority and command more than gentle persuasion. He was inflexible, often rude. His attitude was reminiscent of bygone days, when Spain had ruled the Islands and Catholic priests had been masters. No wonder he was anti-American. The United States had brought in the idea of religious liberty. In the minds of many priests like him, especially those trained in Catholic-dominated lands, religious liberty is a form of heresy. It was not so with me. The First Amendment to the Constitution of the United States reads in part, "Congress shall make no law respecting an establishment of religion, or prohibiting the free exercise thereof." There is also religious freedom in the Philippines, even though it is directly opposed by the hierarchy and teachings of the Roman Catholic church. Pope Leo XIII wrote, "It is not lawful to demand, to defend, or to grant unconditional freedom of thought, or speech, or writing, or religion, as if these were so many rights given by nature to man. . . . Although on account of the extraordinary political conditions [of today] it usually happens that the church acquiesces in certain modern liberties, not because she prefers them in themselves, but because she judges it expedient that they should be permitted."[17]

---

[17]Boettner, p. 417; Cecil John Cadoux, *Roman Catholicism and Freedom,* 4th ed. (London: Independent Press, 1947), p. 31.

The Italian priest was jealous of my successes, and for some reason I became afraid of him. I was happy, therefore, that there was another American priest in Baler, a good friend of mine from seminary days.

In Baler, the Carmelites were in charge of eighty villages. My job was to cover these villages on foot and by jeep, boat, and horseback. Besides covering these mini-parishes, I said daily mass, heard confessions, visited church members, and taught a class in the high school.

The place I enjoyed most was Dibut Bay. From the first time I went there I found its people exceptionally attractive. They were a shy people with a simple, happy lifestyle that would be the envy of city dwellers. Dibut Bay itself is the picture romanticists dream about: warm nights, long stretches of white, sandy beaches, bouquets of tropical flowers, and palm trees heavy with coconuts. My purpose in going there was to introduce the natives to Christianity; each morning that I was there I offered mass and a few words of religious instruction under a coconut tree.

They never questioned me when I told them that baptism was necessary for salvation and that Christ was in the Host when I pronounced certain words over the bread and wine. I never said anything about repentance or about their acceptance of Christ as Lord and Saviour. My objective was to place them under the influence of the ceremony of the mass and to woo them by its solemn majesty. I knew that its mysterious qualities and incomprehensible Latin words would fit in with their mystical superstitions. I sought to impress them and gain prestige for the church by explaining that we had come from a land thousands of miles away so that we might help them and bring them the knowledge of God. We did not need to explain anything about the church, for they did not question. We sought to build habits of attendance, submission, and obedience, especially at the most important points in their lives: birth, marriage, festivals, and death. Eventually the rest would take care of itself.

Then one day my brother American Carmelite priest was transferred to another post. In his place a Filipino diocesan priest came to Baler. We both agreed that the senior pastor did not like us and was especially jealous of our popularity. His dictatorial manner and harshness frequently aroused resentment among the people. I recall the day a Filipino came to the rectory in rage and pounded on the door so furiously that I thought he would break it down before I could get it open. He had come to kill the Italian priest, who had refused to baptize the baby of his second wife. To calm him down, I promised to baptize the baby secretly, but this failed to soothe his anger or stop his threats to kill the priest. I forced the door closed and locked it, then got the houseboy to climb out the back window and go for the police. I ran upstairs to the trembling priest, who had heard the threats, and helped him hide in the attic. The police arrived before anything more serious happened. From that time on, my relationship with the Italian improved a little, but we never became friends.

More than a year before, when I had knelt before the bishop in Washington, D. C., I had promised to serve God without any reservation. I would exemplify detachment, self-abnegation, and piety. That seemed wonderful while I was a novice in Brookline, but it was not working for me in Baler. My health began to fail. The lack of variety in the diet emaciated me, and I weakened as I lost weight. The only time we ate properly was when Bishop Shanley paid us a visit, and that was only once a year. Then we had vegetables, ham, and plenty of liquor.

The students at Mount Carmel High School were my greatest joy in Baler. They gave a new dimension of joy and usefulness to my life, and I was especially proud of my classes. It was here that human nature began to assert itself. Almost unconsciously, I started favoring one of my students. She was a beautiful young woman, and an excellent conversationalist. Of all my students, she was the one I most enjoyed talking to. Occasionally she stayed after class to ask questions or discuss something I had said during a lecture. After a while it became apparent that our friendship was becoming very important both to me and to her. I looked for her when the student body poured out of school. I searched the congregation before I said mass, to see if she was there. When I preached or conducted a novena down by the seashore, I longed for her presence. If she wasn't there, I felt alone.

One afternoon, when classes were finished, I was collecting books that had been left on the desks. She walked in and began helping me. We had just finished placing the books on a shelf when I turned to say something to her. My heart leaped and I was suddenly transfixed by the tender look of love I saw in her eyes. Time seemed to stop as my eyes drank in her beautiful smile. She must have read the same thing in my eyes at that moment, for she moved closer, and I took her in my arms and drew her to me. As I held her and kissed her, a rhapsody of joy filled my whole being. She left a few minutes later, but my heart went with her.

I had never had a date; I had never kissed a girl; I had never even held hands with one, but now I felt that I loved her. Even then I was afraid to believe it. I didn't really know what love was. I had never written a love letter, but now I began writing to her, and to my great joy, she responded with her own love letters. Still, I wondered how a priest who holds Christ every morning during mass could hold a woman in his arms and tenderly say, "I love you." Suddenly my calling wasn't enough. I was filled with fear and consternation. I couldn't understand it, no matter how I tried.

For a Filipino in a small town, a relationship like ours meant just one thing: marriage! My behavior was comparable to a marriage proposal. I was too naive to realize that I had obligated myself; my judgment became blurred, and I feebly tried to explain to Nita that a Catholic could never be happily married to a priest. Love frightened me. I began to back off. Then her father, a public school teacher and an inactive Catholic, entered the picture. "Father," he said, "you love my daughter. She loves you. It's that simple. Why don't you marry her?" I answered nothing. I was too shocked. Forsake the priesthood? Forsake my vows? Bring a scandal to my church, my family, my friends, and the Carmelite order? Never!

Little did I know that Baler was buzzing with a rumor that Nita and I would soon marry. Bishop Shanley, down in the town of Infanta, heard the rumor—thanks to a jealous church secretary, who hated Nita and who told the senior pastor, the Italian priest. He hurried to tell the bishop, who wasted no time in coming to Baler in his yacht. After greetings, he invited me aboard his yacht for a day of fishing. I accepted the invitation with the greatest pleasure.

We spent most of the day fishing in Dibut Bay, but when the fishing was done, he turned away from Baler and headed to Infanta. It was not until we arrived at his headquarters that I realized his real purpose. "I have heard that you are going to marry," he said.

I was embarrassed and became somewhat indignant. I replied, "Your Excellency, I have an affection for the young lady. I can't deny that. I don't know why I feel the way I do, but I assure you that I have no intention of getting married."

I hadn't been in his office more than ten minutes when he told me that I would not be returning to Baler. He told me that I was being sent back to the monastery at Holy Hill.

His order struck me like a thunderbolt. I was too stunned to protest. My personal effects, even my colorful and expensive chasuble, had to remain behind. My mother had given me this vestment to wear over other garments when offering mass. He denied me the opportunity to explain to anyone, even to Nita, my friends in Baler, or the Italian priest. In two days I was out of the Philippines. I had lost face completely, and my reputation was tarnished.

Nita's enemy and the Italian priest had done their work. Perhaps Bishop Shanley felt that he had to do what he did. That was bad enough, but even worse was the humiliation when I reached home. I thought of the shame I had brought on my mother, who had sacrificed so much for me, and on my brother, who held me in such high esteem. I felt that I was a criminal because I had fallen in love with a woman. I pictured the Carmelites snickering to themselves. My image and career were damaged, and though my mother and brother expressed their understanding and concern, I knew they were ashamed. When the Carmelites at Holy Hill acted as if they didn't know a thing, the humiliation was even worse. I knew that they knew, but no one commented, and I worried about what was in their hearts.

The real struggle came when I tried to settle down to monastic life. I grieved about the way things had been handled. I was young; I had worked hard in Baler and had done a good job. I was willing to stay in the Philippines, and I felt that the bishop could at least have relocated me to another part of the Islands. In a sense I had been exiled, branded, and returned to the Carmelites like unwanted merchandise. My dismissal had been handled roughly, even without the approval of Father Albert, my own provincial at Holy Hill.

I had been one of Father Albert's most exemplary students, but I felt that I was far less now. I knew that he saw the rebellion in my heart, so I tried to excise it by prayer and contemplation.

I tried to understand the reasons; I began to see that my discontent had commenced shortly after my arrival in the Philippines. The recitation of the breviary, the meditation, and formal prayers had become dry rigamaroles like stagnating repetitions of poetry. The feeling of God's presence during celebration of the masses had become less real, and I had begun to see it as mere formality and tradition lacking spiritual reality. I saw in the actions of other priests an attitude similar to my own. Still, I prayed and tried to recapture the feelings I had once known. I tried to heal my hurt by remembering that I had violated the rigid orthodoxy of monastic life, but that didn't help. I began to feel like the gaunt skeletons of the burned-out buildings in Manila: the walls were there, but there was no life in them. I began to understand why so many priests on the mission field set aside such practices as saying the Divine Office. Even my religious habit, which I had previously worn with such fierce pride and distinction, was beginning to chafe.

Fear kept me from expressing my doubts, just as it does many priests and nuns. Could I admit that I might have been wrong? I asked myself, "Is it not arrogance to question the one apostolic church? How dare I challenge centuries of theologians by questioning anything I have been taught? Am I not risking excommunication? Might I be called a Judas? Or declared anathema?" Even on the practical side I wondered what I was prepared to do outside the church. I had been trained, but I had not been educated. I began to realize how far I had been sequestered away from the truth about the Bible and the world around me. I was a prisoner, a living dead man, encased in a tomb that I myself had helped build. Life seemed to have less meaning for me with every passing day.

9 Windows to Truth

"Bart, your problem is simple," a Catholic friend said. "Your longing for love has become more important to you than your priestly vows. Think about it."

That jolted me. If that was all there was to my growing concern and doubts about the Catholic church, then I was no more than a fault-finding hypocrite. I wondered how others felt; from time to time I discussed my feelings with fellow priests, not as an adversary of the church but as one seeking reassurance. What surprised me most was that they could not help.

Catholic priests in general have a high threshold of tolerance. Their stoic endurance, spirit of sacrifice, and courageous perseverance have always impressed me. I don't remember many priests complaining that they were hungry, tired, or cold—even when I knew them to be. But there were few who didn't complain about celibacy. I learned that from the 1940s till now, more and more priests have been unwilling to accept the lonely stagnation of bachelorhood—dying old, alone, and heirless. Many find their loneliness as bitter as gall.

Perhaps my experience in the Philippines was the greatest blessing of my life, because even against my will the scales of blindness were being lifted from my eyes and the windows to truth were being edged open. But I was stubborn and stiff-necked. For example, when a friend pointed out contradictions between Christ's teachings and Catholic dogma, I blanked him out and refused to have anything further to do with him. When someone told me that the dogma of purgatory has no basis in Scripture, I refused to listen and gave his words no more thought than I would to a dry leaf rustling in the breeze. I was caught in the labyrinth of Catholic doctrine and traditions.

At night, after prayers, I lay down and kissed the brown scapular, but I found no peace. Oftentimes sleep would not come as I tossed, tormented by questions and doubt.

I knew I wouldn't find the answers at Holy Hill. I wanted to get away from there as soon as possible.

I went to the father provincial, at one time my novice master in Brookline, to see about the possibility of going into the Navy Chaplain Corps. His first question was, "Do you have any intention of seeing that young lady in the Philippines in the event you go into the service and are sent to the Far East?" Very matter-of-factly I answered, "Why yes, of course." That was it. The provincial then and there denied my request. Knowing my addiction to sports, however, he suggested that I coach a Catholic high school football team or take a position in a minor seminary. I declined. Then I heard that the Spanish Carmelites in Arizona needed help. Arizona! I liked that idea.

A few weeks later I left the quiet cloister of Holy Hill for a little town in northeast Arizona, high in the mountains, near one of the largest copper mines in America. I was appointed as assistant pastor to a senior Hungarian Carmelite at Holy Cross parish, and I soon found out that my work was cut out for me. I was to work in an amiable Chicano community. It didn't take long before I was labeled "the gringo priest." Father Pat Perjes was a great man to work with, and although neither of us could speak Spanish, we loved the people and they loved us. I found that the Hispanic people, very remarkable for their intelligence, endurance, and goodness, were a great credit to America; but I also saw that as far as the Roman Catholic church was concerned, they were less important than the richer segments of our society. It pained me to learn that since 1940, in Texas alone, two million had left Romanism for Protestant churches, and that in southern

California thousands more had left the religion of their ancestors. I was determined to do whatever I could to reverse that trend.

I visited families and classrooms, sat on the bench during high school football games, and even sat with parishioners on street corners sharing a glass of buttermilk or a beer. I felt happy that I was accomplishing something for the church.

Then bad news came. The bishop in Tucson took several parishes in the state away from the Spanish Carmelites. The reason was that most of the Carmelites came from Barcelona, Spain, and an astonishing number were leaving the priesthood for the freedom and opportunities they saw in America.

My new assignment took me to St. Margaret's in Tucson, where to my surprise I was given no specific responsibilities other than to say mass, make a few hospital calls at nearby St. Mary's Hospital, hear a confession now and then, and call on a few parishioners. It disturbed me deeply that I was not put to better use for the church and that my volunteer efforts were discouraged.

I knelt before the Blessed Sacrament and asked the Blessed Virgin for help, but the heavens seemed as brass. I went to distant parishes, where I unloaded my burden in confession, but the priests usually advised me to "pray more and get out on the golf course a little more." My dissatisfaction grew; when I saw that things were not likely to improve in Arizona, I sought a new assignment. I heard of a need in San Diego, California. The idea of going to that city, working in a parish, and thereby being able to provide for my widowed mother gave me hope for tomorrow. A visit to the bishop of San Diego, some canonical paperwork, and finally a two-hundred-dollar stipend to the chancery office, and I belonged to the diocese.

It was my good fortune to be sent to Blessed Sacrament, a large, smoothly operated parish with no apparent problems. I could not have asked for a better atmosphere to solve my identity crisis. Monsignor Francis Ott, the pastor, well known and respected in the diocese, became a friend. I worked hard at Blessed Sacrament, and for a while I felt that I had reached the proper place for God's service.

I dreamed of preaching like Bishop Fulton J. Sheen. He was one of my heroes. His sensitive, aristocratic face and his gentle manner and smile projected a fatherly love that drew millions to their television sets and made them want to know him better. He didn't shout or use histrionics to impress his hearers, but he could take the most ordinary subject and raise it to high drama. He was also a master at using a blackboard and chalk to outline his subject. I recall one evening when he raised this question: "Why are so many men and women unkind to their own families while they are pleasant and considerate toward others?" His answer was as startlingly simple as it was true: "It's because they can get away with it; the family has to take it!" Some speakers would have talked thirty minutes without answering the question; he had the remarkable ability to hold a mirror up to the world and make people see truths about themselves, even when those truths were unpleasant.

I read his books, listened to his radio messages, attended his Lenten series in Washington, D. C., and watched his television programs. I wanted to reach people the way he did, but my efforts fell far short of the mark. My "homilies" lacked conviction. My ten-minute, candy-coated sermonettes had no content. "Justification" and "sanctification" were not part of my vocabulary. I had a pleasant social message but not God's anointing power. I was conducting a mechanical ministry because I had grown cold and indifferent.

As former priest L. H. Lehmann writes, "It takes but a few short years of the mechanized ministry of Roman church law and practice to cool that zealous enthusiasm of Christian ideals to the gray ashes of utter indifference and the carelessness of deep despair."[18]

One lovely spring morning when the pastor, his assistant, the secretary, and the housekeeper were gone, I decided to throw my few belongings into my car and leave everything for good. My first stop was my mother's place. I knew that I could reason with her and that she wouldn't brand me a sinner merely because I wanted to leave the priesthood. One thing I

---

[18] *The Soul of a Priest* (New York: Loizeaux Brothers, 1938), pp. 43-44.

could expect, however, was that she would bring God into the picture. But when I told her, she only said, "Son, the Lord wants you to follow Him completely. Learn of Him. Remember His mercy and goodness in permitting you to be a priest." What she said and the way she said it persuaded me to return to the rectory to pray more about the whole matter and reconsider what I should do with my life.

I was able to get back to the parish and unpack before the others returned. I settled down and counted my blessings. I had wonderful friends at Blessed Sacrament. Monsignor Ott and John Portman were fine priests and pleasant to work with. Some priests in the diocese were quite dedicated. Some were members of religious orders. Was it not possible for me to feel at home? Many of these fine priests have since left the priesthood, and as I later learned, the San Diego diocese is known as a *refugium peccatorum*, ("refuge for sinners")—a place for problem priests.

I was surprised one day when Monsignor Ott told me that there was a former priest in our parish and that he wanted me to salvage him. This ex-priest had a wife and daughter.

"Bart," the monsignor said, "I want you to win this man back to the priesthood. He is going to mass; he is still a Catholic; but he has to come back to the priesthood. He has a brother who is a priest somewhere in the Midwest who wants him to leave his family and return to the priesthood, where he belongs."

My mouth was dry when I promised the monsignor that I would do my very best.

Up to this time I had heard that ex-priests were lunatics, drunks, heretics, and, of course, "skirt chasers," but I had never seen an "ex." I had the impression that resigned priests have two horns and a tail. Now I was curious; I would see for myself. That evening I went to visit the former priest. When I rang the doorbell I was greeted by his wife, who wouldn't allow me to come in the house. I sensed that she knew who I was even though I didn't wear my Roman collar. I did get him to leave the house and talk with me for a few minutes, but he felt the rectory was a better place to talk.

"Whatever it is, I will come to see you," he said.

After one meeting, I had him convinced that he should leave his wife and daughter and return to the priesthood. I suggested that he go to Via Coeli: ("The Way to Heaven"), a sort of religious San Quentin for wayward priests, located near Santa Fe, New Mexico. I became proud of my ability to persuade him to leave his family for rehabilitation.

"Father," he said, "my wife is a registered nurse. She and our daughter have a lovely home. My wife is financially secure, and I am in a good position to leave them and return to my priestly duties. My brother, a priest, comes here every year begging me to 'Come home.' Now I am ready."

"Ed," I said, "God will bless you for this move. Let's keep in touch." The visit was short and decisive.

I suppose I couldn't believe in my secret heart that a former priest would actually leave his family and return. So after several months passed I called his home to see whether he had actually gone to Via Coeli. To my surprise, he answered the phone. "Ed, this is Bart," I began. "I thought you had left."

He hesitated a moment, then replied, "Bart, I mean Father Bart, I just couldn't get myself to do it. I've been on the run for years. I couldn't leave my wife and daughter."

As we said goodbye and I hung up the phone, I smiled and said to myself, "Thank God, he's not stupid!"

Thirteen years later when I returned to San Diego with a wife and son, I looked up this former priest. I had an apology to make. As he opened the door, I said, "Ed, do you remember me? I'm an ex-priest now. I too have a family, and I have come to ask you to forgive me for trying to get you to leave your family and return to the priesthood." He looked at me for a long time, then tears filled his eyes. "I forgave you long ago, Bart. My wife died of cancer some years ago, and my daughter is a grown woman. She is in the kitchen now, and I want to ask you to say nothing that will give away my secret. You see, I have never told her that I was a priest. I am afraid to tell her. It's something I can never do! She has asked me many times about past years, but I never have explained. I'm afraid she would hate me if she knew. I couldn't take that." Tears were running down his face as we parted.

My heart went out to him. What awful fears we have of one another! I have seen and talked to him since that time, and my heart goes out to him, for he is still hiding his secret, burdened with guilt and heart-breaking fear. He punishes himself without reason. He lives in limbo, fearing to speak of his past, fearing to meet others who might expose his secret, wondering if his torment will continue beyond the grave. Perhaps his daughter already knows, but she is afraid to say anything—so there is a wall between them, a wall that may never come down. I have often prayed for him, knowing that if only he would believe the words of Jesus, he would be renewed with unspeakable joy and glory. For Jesus said, "I am the way, the truth, and the life: no man cometh unto the Father, but by me" (John 14:6). And did Jesus not say, "If the Son therefore shall make you free, ye shall be free indeed" (John 8:36)?

At Blessed Sacrament parish I had time to think about the future. I had often heard of Catholic chaplains who did great things aboard aircraft carriers and in the jungles of Iwo Jima and Guadalcanal. I remembered the famed Irish priest and chaplain, Willie Doyle, who died in the front lines during World War I. He was a hero, a leader, and a shepherd. I wanted to be like him, if possible. I wanted to serve in an active way. So one day I made an appointment to see the bishop. I asked permission to serve as a chaplain in the United States Navy. The bishop gave me his blessing and said that I would make a great chaplain. I was elated as I returned to my parish to complete one year in San Diego before joining the navy.

When I entered the navy, I met and talked with Protestant clergymen for the first time. I worked with Lutherans, Presbyterians, Methodists, Baptists, and Pentecostals. Even though there were only three Catholic priests among two dozen Protestant chaplains in the Navy Chaplain's School, we felt superior in every way, especially when it came to theology. On the surface there was much camaraderie, but when the three of us got together, we referred to Protestant chaplains as "P.B.'s"—Protestant bastards. Yet somehow they seemed different. They were more serious about their calling than we were.

Of course, my mother felt uneasy about my being in the navy. She feared that it was too worldly, but we both felt that my working among service people and ministering to Catholic servicemen would be a privilege and would help me find contentment.

It was a very exciting day when we chaplains received our first set of orders. I was sent to the Oak Knoll Naval Hospital in Oakland, California. I hoped that I would soon be sent to the Far East, not as a Carmelite with the vow of poverty, but as a chaplain with rank. I saw that socializing was expected of chaplains—especially Catholic chaplains, since they had no families. Cocktail parties, pretty flirting nurses, and professional sailors made life interesting. But the other Catholic chaplains around the naval district began to see that I was a "straight arrow" priest. I didn't drink or chase women (my mother was living with me then), and I attended strictly to duty. Up till then my mother had always had an exalted opinion of priests, but then both she and I began to see that they were human, often frivolous, demonstrating a zest for life, often with the candle alight at both ends. As I watched the Roman chaplains wine and dine during the week, then get away for a weekend at Carmel or Las Vegas, I began to realize that many priests were social workers by day and playboys by night. Hearing their confessions reinforced this fact, and again I realized that the rampant immorality among the Catholic hierarchy was largely attributable to the confessional. These priests heard so many confessions about unchaste behavior that some began to generalize, thinking that every town and village is another Peyton Place. Of course they were wrong in thinking this, but the fact remains that many priests believed it, and many young, virile men simply responded to occasions of opportunity. It is not unusual for young women to "get a crush" on young priests and ministers.

After a year at Oak Knoll, I was promoted to lieutenant and given a set of orders for the 1st Marine Air Wing, Atsugi, Japan. That was just what I wanted; I was thrilled as I read my orders and saw that I would have a week's leave in Hawaii and ten days in Tokyo before reporting to the Marine Air Wing.

I had never had a date in my life, but now the thought of meeting an attractive young woman became very exciting. I was walking on the Ginza in Tokyo one day and saw a beautiful Japanese lady. Without effort, I walked up to her and said, "Please excuse me, but I would like to meet you. My name is Bart. And your name?" That was the first of many dates I had with Mineko. She had no idea that I was military, nor did she dream that I was a Catholic priest.

The excitement of reporting to the Marine Air Wing paled into insignificance in comparison to seeing Mineko. I thought her the most beautiful woman I had ever seen. Several times each week I took a train from Atsugi to Tokyo to see her at Nicola's Pizza Place or to have dinner with her in some beautiful restaurant. There was something peaceful, serene, and radiant about this young woman. After several months of dating, we met for lunch one cold January afternoon. Her curiosity and persistent questioning as to who I was finally compelled me to tell her that I was a priest. It took a little while for this to sink in; then she said, "I knew that there was something very different about you."

A beautiful romance was budding, but that came to a sudden halt when I unexpectedly received orders to Futema, a helicopter base in Okinawa. I didn't like that, although I wondered whether God was trying to tell me something.

My life in the "Paradise of the Pacific" was relatively quiet until another Catholic chaplain from Oak Knoll reported to my station. The monastery had trained me well, and I was never a "night person"; the new chaplain, however, was just the opposite. He loved the nights, the dances, the visits to clubs, and the opportunities to practice his charms with the ladies. Together we often visited the officers' clubs at Naha Air Base, where we became good friends with the C-130 pilots and their wives and girl friends. "Pat" had given me special instructions before we set foot on Naha Air Base. "Bart, let everybody know you are a priest. But not me. Let me play the part of a psychologist." He did this very successfully and with great humor until one day several officers' wives caught him wearing the cross on his uniform at another air base on the island. Pat never lived that down.

Everybody thought it was great joke—except Pat.

I prided myself on being a "regular Joe" on Okinawa. The more worldly I appeared, the more Catholics and Protestants flocked to my masses. I felt sorry for the Baptist chaplain, Kenneth R. Gordon. He never seemed to have any fun, and there was always that big black Bible lying on his desk. He actually preached out of that Bible, and his men sang hymns of praise and redemption. I watched in astonishment as rugged marines and navy men went to church carrying their Bibles! We Catholics never did that! I thought, "That poor chaplain: he's missing all the fun."

Years later, after my conversion, I had an opportunity to preach for him in his church. He told me that during those days on Okinawa, he had felt sorry for me!

He expressed it all in a letter he later wrote me, which he called "Recollections on Bartholomew Brewer:"

Chaplain Brewer came across to me as a typical "religious" Roman Catholic priest. He rigidly adhered to the works and practices of his church. He refused to be deterred from reading his daily religious guide. At times I was not sure whether to be jealous or angry, for I felt he used his religious devotions and requirements as an excuse to get out of some unpleasant work—work that pertained to his areas of responsibility but that I had to perform because he was too busy with his "religious exercises"! I wished he would spend at least some of his time reading the Bible.

The most important part of Chaplain Brewer's day was his daily mass. As I observed his meticulous daily preparation and participation, I saw an emerging mechanical process of form and ritual that appeared to be more important than any message from God's Word. Personally, I could see little worth in it, except to give the chaplain and people a "religious feeling" and a false sense of security with God, based not on any real personal commitment but on just the mechanical duty of "doing." My heart went out for Bart's salvation, but he was always too busy for more than superficial or official conversation.

One of the most enjoyable times in my life and ministry was our [Protestant] Sunday services, especially the opportunity to preach the Word and explain God's will for our lives. On the other hand, Chaplain Brewer's sermons were generally of the "five minute" variety, admonishing his hearers to be good, to have faith, and other nice ideas that anyone could practice if he tried, but with no observable biblical basis. Often his message was from an official church guide, not from the Word of God. How I wished that he knew and would preach the Word instead.

One program we shared together stands out in my memory. I had spent several months in arduous preparation for the completion and furnishing of a new chapel, and it was time for the dedication service. As Air Facility chaplain, I was directed to prepare this program, contact the various participants, and make appropriate arrangements for all personnel and materials. Of course I asked our Roman Catholic chaplain to have a part. Initially he declined, saying it was "not necessary." I pointed out that the chapel was built for both Protestants and Catholics and that since he was the Roman Catholic chaplain for the base, it was only right that he have a part. He agreed but asked that his part be minor. Thinking that Roman Catholic priests were known for their benedictions, I asked Bart to take the closing portion, and he agreed. Shortly thereafter he bewildered me and intrigued my wondering mind by asking me if I knew of a good benediction! I suggested the Aaronic Benediction ("The Lord bless thee and keep thee . . ."). He acknowledged that as a good choice and further startled me by asking if I had a book in which it was to be found so he could make a copy! I showed the passage to him in my Protestant Bible, and he made a copy. On the day of dedication, I chuckled when Bart could not find his typewritten card and borrowed my Protestant Bible, from which he read the benediction.

My wife and I tried on numerous occasions to have Bart visit our home for supper, but he always seemed to *have another appointment. After being turned down each time, albeit graciously and with an appearance of deepest appreciation, we felt that he had no intention of ever accepting our hospitality. We concluded that he did not care to eat with us, though he never gave any hint of such an attitude. It took us a number of years to discover that his refusals were founded on wariness of our spiritual intentions and his concern over our possible attempt to "convert" him.*

I felt sorry for Bart, for I believed that if he ever became a born-again Christian as dedicated to Jesus Christ as he was to his church, he would make a real impact on many lives. I saw him as one living in bondage to a system and under the cover of spiritual darkness while feeling smugly and defiantly secure. I always felt an unspoken attitude on Bart's part that "the Catholic church has the only way to God. We are totally right; you are wrong and lost!"

I did not realize at that time that his expertise and confidence were not really based on knowledge of the Bible or spiritual depth, but on philosophy and sociology. I found that other chaplains at the base were also confused by his authoritarian manner and pronouncements based on these educational disciplines. I was somewhat awed by Bart and his priestly associates because I had a fear of Roman Catholic priests. From childhood I had been awed by their long, mysterious black robes and the attitude of authority they displayed.

After Bart received orders to return to another duty station back in the States, we tried to communicate with him, but he never returned more than a brief greeting, ignoring all our questions about his status and plans. What he would not tell us until years later was that he was grappling with spiritual questions related to many things that he knew I believed and preached! We never heard from Bart again until several years later. I was completely dumbfounded to find that the man I had known as Father "Black Bart" was applying for a Baptist pastorate!

Apparently a miracle of unspeakable proportions had occurred. "Could it be," I asked myself, "that the epitome of Roman Catholicism has made a personal commitment of his life to Jesus Christ and has been truly born again?"

My query was not resolved until Bart suddenly appeared at our church in Arizona after another lapse of time. He had his wife and son with him. This time we invited him to dinner and Christian fellowship, and he accepted. We had a glorious time!

10 A New Life

After fifteen months of chaplain duty with the navy on Okinawa and in Thailand and Japan, it was time to return home. To my great joy I was assigned to the naval station in Long Beach, California. When I arrived, I found that not much had changed since I had left. Mother was happy that I had adjusted so well to the chaplain corps. My brother, Paul, had married. I was eager to get to work. Mother and I found a comfortable apartment near the base, and I began my routine: saying daily mass, hearing confessions, baptizing babies, providing catechetical instruction for prospective converts, and visiting the sick and bereaved.

Almost every night in our little apartment, Mother and I studied the Scriptures. As I studied, I saw much disagreement between church dogma and the Word of God. Questions kept tugging at my mind: Why? What had caused the church to depart so far from the Scriptures? Why had tradition become more important than simple faith?

I had already begun to doubt the authority of the church, but there was fear in my heart. My world seemed to be crumbling, and sometimes it seemed that the very heavens were shaking. Oftentimes I asked myself, "How dare I, a simple priest from Philadelphia, question the writings of the church fathers, the popes, the martyrs, and the saints?" I had heard of priests who left the church and whose lives were shattered by the load of guilt they bore. Some had retreated into hermitage, forsaking both God and man; not a few had committed suicide.

My spirit was restless and troubled, but now as I searched for truth, I saw that there was no turning back. It was time for a titanic decision.

When I received my honorable discharge from the United States Navy and the movers came to our apartment in Long Beach, Mother and I had our goods sent north, instead of south to San Diego. It was for real; I would not be returning to my diocese.

On our way north, we passed through the little town of Gilroy, not far from San Jose, California. I stopped the car and asked mother to wait. I took my mass kit into the Catholic church and left it next to the confessional booth. The umbilical cord was cut! At last I had done what I knew was right.

I stepped into a new life that day, one I would never have understood or even appreciated had I not left the glamor that once I called life. I turned to the Lord with my whole heart, unfettered by false gods and by false religion. I have never regretted taking that step, not for one moment!

It was 1963, and I was starting all over again. I had no plans except to do God's will. Like many priests, I had been a loner. I had had a wide circle of acquaintances but few friends; there was no one I could turn to for counsel. Moreover, I was incredibly naive; I didn't even know how to make a living.

My mother and I headed north from Gilroy. Since my brother and his wife lived in the Bay Area near San Francisco, I decided that would be as good a place as any to begin a new life. Fortunately, my navy severance pay was enough for me to rent a small apartment we found in the little town of Fairfax, about twenty minutes north of the Golden Gate Bridge.

It didn't take long, however, to see that what money I had would soon be gone, so I got a job selling encyclopedias. The job gave me an opportunity to learn about people in all walks of life. San Francisco is one of the most cosmopolitan cities on earth, and its people are extremely diverse. I worked hard, often till late at night, and proved that I could make a living; in fact, I became a top salesman in our area. Still, my principal goal was full-time service in the Lord's work.

My experience as a book salesman reinforced my determination to serve God and Him only. Many people I met, both successful and unsuccessful, seemed weary, sick at heart, and discouraged. They had personal and domestic problems as well as social and financial ones. Seeking happiness, they rushed to and fro, trying every new fad and entertainment, only to find them all turn to ashes in their mouths.

But what about myself? I had a good intellectual knowledge of God, but I knew that I hadn't experienced His salvation. There was an emptiness, a vacuum, a restlessness in my soul. If I was to be a minister of the gospel, I needed to know more of His grace. My own life had to be changed; I needed regeneration!

It so happened that across the road from where Mother and I lived was a Lutheran church, and one day I worked up enough courage to knock on the pastor's door. I was greeted by a pleasant man. "What may I do for you?" he asked.

I told him that I was a former Roman priest, and after a while he challenged me to consider becoming a Lutheran pastor. I was flattered, of course. He suggested that I investigate several Lutheran seminaries, there being one as close as Berkeley, California. "It's a liberal school," he said, "but you can turn a deaf ear to what you don't want to hear." That precaution dampened my interest in Berkeley, so he suggested that I meet with some Lutheran leaders in their Los Angeles office. I did meet them, but I found them cold and haughty. They were obviously self-satisfied. I learned that the whole Lutheran church was in turmoil, faced with a possible schism between liberals and strict interpreters of God's Word. Some of their ministers seemed to have lost their way to such a degree that they were allowing men of immoral and perverse character to serve in their pulpits. Some were even leaning towards Romanism. I concluded that I would be of little use in their churches.

By this time three major issues were being resolved in my

search for God's will. I would become a Protestant minister; I would avoid the ecumenical movement; and last but most important of all, I would stand on the Bible as my final authority, both in faith and in practice. I was still, however, unconverted.

Mother had joined the Seventh-day Adventist church, and I chuckle now as I recall how she purposely left Adventist literature around the apartment so that I would read it. I did and found it very interesting. I also enjoyed listening to the Adventist television program, "It Is Written."

In the meantime my brother and his wife had moved to Los Angeles, where they urged us to come. We moved and began attending a Seventh-day Adventist church nearby, in Alhambra. I found the people wonderfully refined, kind, and possessed of high moral standards. Even my brother was impressed by a special message we heard on prophecy. There were no confessional booths, no images, no Stations of the Cross, no candles, no smell of incense, and no altar, and the order of worship was inspiring. Then one evening the pastor preached on the Second Coming of Christ. I had never heard a message like that before! And he preached it right out of the Bible!

So I arranged a meeting with the pastor. The more I heard about Adventism from him, the more I was impressed by its wonderful works in the fields of education, medicine, and foreign missions. I joined the church and was baptized by the pastor. He invited me to be on his church staff, and I was soon introduced to the conference leaders in Glendale. A few weeks later I was invited to preach my first sermon in his church.

I shall never forget one Saturday morning shortly after I first preached there. Services were over, and all the people had departed except for two small groups who remained in the church foyer. I was talking with my mother, my brother, his wife, and several friends, when I looked across the foyer and was startled by a young woman standing there whose beauty dazzled me. I must have stared at her a long time, because when I turned my attention back to my own group, they were all staring at me! I had even forgotten what we were talking about. I stammered a moment, trying to regain my place in the conversation, then asked Paul, "Do you see that young lady over there?"

"Yes," he said. "Who is she?"

I said, "I don't know, but I want to tell you something. I'm going to marry her. That young lady is my future wife."

Paul laughed, "Don't you think you ought to be introduced before you break the news to her?"

I agreed, but how was I going to meet her? I hadn't been in the church long enough to know all the members, but I hadn't seen her before, and I guessed that she was a visitor. I was afraid that she would get away without my knowing even her name. Just then, Mother pulled me aside and whispered that she knew the young woman's mother, who attended another Adventist church. An introduction was arranged.

That little episode in the foyer created a sensation. In no time at all, everyone seemed to know about it, and I was offered so much advice that I began to think the whole congregation might be watching when I did meet her. Perhaps because of that, it took me about two weeks to work up enough courage to ask her to have dinner with me. By that time I felt as though I ought to invite the whole congregation to go with us! The pastor was preaching on the imminent return of Christ, with such power and conviction that I was almost afraid the Second Coming would take place before I could get acquainted with Ruth. I wanted to go to Heaven, but not at that particular moment.

Two dates with Ruth and I was deeply in love with her. I took her to my church again and introduced her to everyone I knew. Rumors buzzed that the tall, dark, thin former priest was serious about taking Ruth for his wife. I didn't have to tell my friends. They knew, I suppose, by simply watching me.

One sunny afternoon, only three weeks after I met her, we took a ride to a small park in the foothills near La Crescenta. I wanted to tell Ruth of my love for her but I didn't know how to begin. We passed a huge billboard advertising Mexican food. Ruth pointed to it and said, "I love Mexican food."

"Do you know what I love?" I asked.

"What?" she asked.

"You." I said.

At that moment my poor little car overheated and started coughing and sputtering, blowing off the radiator cap and spewing water all over the windshield. Fortunately we were near shade trees; I stopped to let the car cool down.

There was a period of painful silence, and I tried to start all over again. "Did you hear what I said back there?" I asked.

She nodded.

Then I said, "Ruth, I love you."

The look in her beautiful brown eyes told me that she loved me too. I wasn't sure what to say next, nor did she say anything. We sat there in silence, then I tried to start the car again. This time it seemed able to go, so we drove farther toward the park and I told her that arrangements had been made for me to go to the Seventh-day Adventist Seminary in Berrien Springs, Michigan, to study the Bible and the teachings of Adventism. I asked her if she would like to go with me.

I guess she could hardly believe what I was getting at. "What do you mean?" she asked.

"You know what I mean."

"No, I don't know."

This went back and forth a few times until she said, "Well, go ahead and say whatever you're trying to say."

Finally, I asked, "Will you marry me?" It was her turn to be speechless. The seconds ticked by as slowly as hours. I don't remember exactly how she said, "Yes," but the important thing to me is that she did.

I recalled that our teachers in the Catholic seminary used to say, "For every man, God created a woman. She's out there, somewhere, waiting for you. Watch out if you do meet her!" Of course such statements were meant as warnings: run! detour! head for the nearest exit if you see her! Now I laughed as I recalled those things.

I had met her at the right time and in the right place, and she was the right girl for me.

Later, I stammered my way through a conversation with her parents, asking their consent. They gave it graciously, and we set a wedding date that would forever be a double holiday for us, July 4th (though it hardly meant Independence Day for the two of us!).

To this day I am amazed that the Lord permitted our paths to cross, then turn and run parallel, as we have helped each other and countless others along the road to salvation and eternal life.

We wanted a quiet wedding. When the pastor heard the news, however, he wanted to announce it to the whole congregation; consequently our plans changed. The congregation began to plan a special wedding. Naturally, both Ruth and I were concerned about the expenses of a large wedding, but the pastor graciously assured us that everything would be taken care of. How marvelously generous those wonderful people were!

The following week, the ladies of the church gave Ruth a shower. She was offered three formal bridal gowns to choose from. One of the ladies offered to direct the wedding, and others volunteered to take care of the flowers, the reception, and everything else that had to be done. It was an instant wedding—planned from start to finish in one night. Exciting days were filled with shopping for all the things needed for such an occasion—dresses for bridesmaids, gifts, cake, punch, everything necessary for a large reception—all those things that most men, especially ex-priests, would never think of.

I could hardly believe it! I, an ex-priest who had conducted so many weddings, was to be the bridegroom! It seemed incomprehensible!

At our wedding Ruth looked like an angel in her beautiful wedding gown. As I looked at the bride I was taking before the altar, my heart was filled with love and pride. Everything was done with grace and beauty.

Two months after our wedding, Ruth and I traveled to Berrien Springs, where I began my studies for the ministry. Both of us had a heavy schedule of classes. Ruth was a senior in Andrews University, and I was in the seminary. There were courses that opened the Bible up to me more than I had ever known before. I learned more about the Bible there in twelve months than I had learned in all my years in Catholic seminaries. Ruth and I worked and prayed, and being far from our parents in California, we had ample time to learn and adjust to our new lives together.

During my studies I was especially impressed by Dr. Edward Heppenstall's course, "Righteousness By Faith." It was in that course, taught from the Apostle Paul's letters to the Romans and Galatians, that I understood what really constitutes salvation. The Law shows us what sinners we are and proves our inability to keep the Law. Christ fulfilled the Law; He bore the curse of our sins and their penalty for me and the whole world!

When Ruth and I were first married, we both had the impression that I was saved. I had been good, I had done right, and if anyone was entitled to salvation by good works, I was. Ruth saw that I had an intellectual knowledge of salvation, but she could also see that I lacked the personal presence of Christ in my heart. I was not deeply interested in personal devotion. I never spoke of what Christ was doing in my life. It was always the church and what it was doing.

One day in 1964, she asked me, "Bart, exactly when did you become a Christian?" My reply was almost indignant. "Why?" I asked. I told her, "I was born a Christian." Right there we both knew that something was wrong. She followed it up with other questions: "Bart, when did Jesus become your Lord and Saviour? When did you consciously receive Him into your life? When did you surrender your will to Him completely and turn your life over to Him?"

I told her that besides being baptized, I had always believed in God. From childhood I had been taught that Jesus died for my sins. I had turned my life over to Him when I first went to Holy Hill. I told her that that should be evident to anyone. I tried to explain that nobody would have gone through all that time in seminaries and monasteries and then have been a priest for ten years without knowing that Christ died for sinners.

At first I didn't admit my error to her, but I soon began to see it. I wanted to substitute my own righteousness and my good works for the imputed righteousness of Christ. Like many Roman Catholics, I failed to realize that mere mental assent or intellectual acceptance does not constitute the surrender of one's heart and life to Christ. Intellectual knowledge alone does not rescue man from his lost estate. I was like a man who knows a great deal about a country but who is not a citizen of it.

Now I saw that man obtains forgiveness and is declared righteous not through the sacraments or through any religious institution, but through Christ, Who was "obedient unto death, even the death of the cross" (Philippians 2:8). It was gloriously simple. As the Apostle Paul wrote, "For the preaching of the cross is to them that perish foolishness; but unto us which are saved it is the power of God" (I Corinthians 1:18). Christ took our place on Calvary. As it is written, "I am crucified with Christ: nevertheless I live; yet not I, but Christ liveth in me: and the life which I now live in the flesh I live by the faith of the Son of God, who loved me, and gave himself for me" (Galatians 2:20). Those wonderful words, "The just shall live by faith," thrilled my soul, and again I read, "For by grace are ye saved through faith; and that not of yourselves: it is the gift of God: Not of works, lest any man should boast" (Ephesians 2:8-9).

One glorious day while I was still in the seminary, the Holy Spirit through God's Word caused me to ask Jesus Christ to wash my sins away in His shed blood. There I repented of my sin. It was there that I received Christ as my Lord and Saviour. I saw that my own works were "as filthy rags" in His sight (Isaiah 64:6). My intellectual achievements were nothing. I renounced my own self-righteousness for His true righteousness. The work of my salvation was finished at Calvary.

There was nothing sensational, dramatic, or highly emotional about my conversion. There was the calm assurance that I was no longer dead in trespasses and sin but that I had been made alive with Christ, raised up to a new life in Him. From the depths of my soul, I knew Whom I believed!

Since that day I have had inner peace and joy, knowing that the chains that bound me are gone forever. I am free! My citizenship is in Heaven! I have become a child of the King. I am forever joined unto the Lord. This was His will for me:

that I might know Him on a personal basis as my ransom, my Lord, and my Saviour.

O, how I wish that I could tell all my Catholic friends that His grace is sufficient. It is not a spiritual prescription via the sacraments. I would cry out to them that the Bible is not an obscure and mysterious book. It is complete and completely inspired: it is God's Word, setting forth the plan of salvation. Scripture "is profitable for doctrine, for reproof, for correction, for instruction in righteousness" (II Timothy 3:16).

My Bible, 'tis a book divine
Where heavenly truth and mercy shine
And wisdom speaks in every line
It speaks to thee; it speaks to me.

My Bible, here with joy I trace
The record of redeeming grace,
Glad tidings for a sinful race,
Good news for thee; good news for me.

My Bible, in this book alone
I find God's holy will made known,
And here His love to man is shown
His love for thee; His love for me.

—Mrs. C. E. Foster

11 The Seventh-day Adventists and Mrs. Ellen G. White

Our little car chugged up the grade to the town of Tujunga, California, where I was to pastor its Seventh-day Adventist church. Once well known as a health resort, Tujunga has lost out in competition with bigger and more luxurious spas, but it is still a delightful place.

The car sighed audibly as we stopped, and I turned off the key in front of a half-century-old building that had once served as a Methodist church. From every viewpoint, it seemed to be crying for care. Broken windows and sills and an accumulation of debris showed signs of vandalism and neglect. Some of its inside walls had never been finished, and the paint was wrinkled and cracked with age, but somehow it had a character that reminded me of a little old-fashioned lady in long skirts and high-buttoned shoes. The sanctuary had been well kept. It was simple and adequate, but on that August day in 1968 the air was still and the building was stifling hot.

Right up to a half hour before the first service was to begin, Ruth and I wondered whether anyone would show up. We hoped for at least a dozen, but to our joyful surprise more than fifty came. Some even brought gifts of fruit, vegetables, and canned goods. It was a very good beginning.

My first sermon emphasized the need for every pastor to preach the good news of salvation and growth in the Lord instead of the sociological drivel that had become popular in many liberal churches. My text was Matthew 4:17—"Repent: for the kingdom of heaven is at hand." As I preached, I saw curiosity about the new minister turn to interest, and interest turn to glowing responsiveness. I was overwhelmed, and it thrilled my soul! Now I was a preacher extolling Christ. No longer was I afraid to preach from the holy Scriptures, as I had been when I was a priest. I no longer had to tread the carpets of fear because I might alienate my bishop by preaching directly from the Bible. I felt the courage of a lion and a renewed commitment. Holy Scripture was my anchor, and His salvation was my message.

I hadn't been ordained as an Adventist minister yet, even though I had completed all study requirements at the Adventist seminary and had served a three-year internship with the White Memorial Seventh-day Adventist Church in Los Angeles.

Several months later the call came for my ordination to take place in the Vallejo Drive Seventh-day Adventist Church in Glendale, and I invited relatives and many friends to join us and share the happy occasion.

Two of us were ordained that day. From the first moment of the service, I could not help contrasting it with my ordination to the Roman Catholic priesthood. There was no pomp or glitter, no singing choirs, no prostration on the floor before the bishop to vow obedience to him and the superiors appointed over us. Instead, it was a simple, edifying service witnessed by a large congregation and many elders of the church. The principal speaker challenged us to serve the Lord with gladness and zeal, reaching out into our communities to bring many into the fold of salvation. My own personal testimony before the assembly was in praise of our Lord and Saviour, for I could declare with Philip, Jesus' disciple, "We have found him, of whom Moses in the law, and the prophets, did write, Jesus of Nazareth, the son of Joseph" (John 1:45). I felt renewed and strengthened in soul and body, and with Ruth at my side I determined to bring the light of the glorious gospel of Christ to all we could reach.

Ordination in Adventism bestows a certain mystique or aura upon its ministers, for they are carefully chosen not only for their dedication and biblical scholarship, but also for the qualities of their personal life, so that they may lead the way by example. The work was demanding in that I had three messages to prepare each week, visits to church members, missionary work in the community, and a multitude of lesser duties. Our joy made our duties seem light, however, and I could say with the great Dwight L. Moody, "I may get tired in the work, but I never get tired of the work."

I admired the Adventists greatly. They were friendly and willing to become involved in church activities. We enthusiastically made plans to refurbish the old building, and volunteer crews assembled regularly to carry them out. Paint brushes flew, windows were repaired, and landscaping commenced. We saw the spirit that built early America renewed in our midst as friends and neighbors worked together in harmony for the good of all. The whole building took on a new appearance, and the congregation grew in both spiritual stature and numbers.

As time passed, there was only one thing that dampened our joy and caused some unrest in my heart. That was the heavy reliance of many Adventists on the writings and teachings of Mrs. Ellen G. White, one of the founders of the church. It seemed a small thing at first, so I made few references to her in my sermons. I had read her book *The Desire of the Ages* and found it inspiring and beautiful, and I gloried in the expectation that Christ's return to earth is drawing near. Even the Adventists' observance of Saturday as the sabbath, the day of rest, seemed innocuous. It was inconvenient, to be sure, since it caused Adventists to suspend all work and business on Saturday and thus be out of step with the community, but I saw no actual wrong in it.

Once each year, the Southern California Conference of the Seventh-day Adventists conducted a seminar called "The Testimony Countdown." Its purpose was to help pastors and their wives understand Mrs. White's teachings. Ruth and I eagerly looked forward to it. We wanted to know all we could about Mrs. White and her messages. At the same time, however, I wanted to be sure that our little flock would look only to the Scriptures as the final authority for their faith. I was opposed to any person of these days who claimed to be a divinely inspired prophet, just as I was to the Catholic church's claims that the writings of its doctors must be accepted as equal in authority to the writings of the apostles.

I knew, of course, that Mrs. White's writings were considered important among Adventists, but at the seminar I learned that leading Adventist elders regard them as equal in authority to the writings of the prophets—Samuel, Daniel, or John the Baptist.[19] The lecturers' teachings dismayed me as we were informed that Mrs. White's prophecies and interpretations are to be accepted as final authority and "free from error." Mrs. White herself apparently thought that her interpretations were infallible. In her book *Testimonies* she wrote, "When I send you a testimony of warning and reproof, many of you declare it to be merely the opinion of Sister White. You have thereby insulted the Spirit of God." She came to regard herself as a sovereign authority on everything to which she put her mind. Disdainful of opinions that differed from hers, she is said to have subjected many visitors to critical cross-examinations to see if they differed from her in even the slightest details. She claimed that what she wrote was directly inspired by God: "I do not write one article in the paper expressing merely my own ideas. They are what God has opened before me in vision."[20]

Yes, I knew Mrs. White's accomplishments, and I knew that her teachings had become central doctrines of the Seventh-day Adventist church, but I could not accept them as being equal with Scripture. Several times I was "called on the carpet" to explain why I continued to neglect Mrs. White's teachings in my sermons. It was rumored that "Pastor Brewer doesn't believe Ellen White's teachings. He never refers to her." Another source of suspicion arose because at the end of every message I gave an invitation to the unsaved to come forward and receive Christ as Lord and Saviour. I was not the

---

[19]Mrs. White herself made statements to this effect; see *Testimonies for the Church* (Mountain View, CA: Pacific Press, 1948), V, p. 661.

[20]*Testimonies for the Church,* V, p. 67.

conventional Adventist minister, but people were coming forward to receive Him publicly, often shedding tears of repentance. Lives were being changed through the preaching of the Word. I looked to no other source than the Bible, but the Adventists wanted more—namely, the mastery of Mrs. White's writings and teachings.

I was summoned to a meeting one day, and certain complaints were brought to my attention. That evening, I told Ruth that some of the charges against me were true but that they all concerned Mrs. White. Even my critics admitted that I was faithful to the Bible. I saw that as long as I questioned Mrs. White's predictions and interpretations, I was headed for repeated confrontations with the church's leaders. The more I thought about it, the more convinced I was that it would be unethical to remain a minister in a church whose doctrines I could not accept.

I would not submit to another pope or modern prophetess. When I was a Catholic priest in one of the strictest orders, I was told that the writings of Saint Thomas Aquinas had to be accepted as doctine; but he treated the Bible as if it were an advisory packet. He taught error and fostered idolatry and pagan tradition. Mrs. White misled people too, although perhaps to a lesser degree. She contradicted the Apostle Paul, who wrote, "I determined not to know any thing among you, save Jesus Christ, and him crucified" (I Corinthians 2:2).

Our decision to leave Adventism was not easy. We loved and appreciated the people. It was in the Adventist seminary that I came to know Christ as my personal Lord and Saviour. It was in this denomination that I met my precious wife. It was in this group that I came to revere the Scriptures, to study, teach, and preach them.

Three times each week I visited the studio of a radio preacher friend to make recordings. It was always a time of fellowship and spiritual nourishment. When I presented my predicament to him, he said, "Bart, don't compromise your position. Your only authority is the Bible. When a church has a questionable relationship to Scripture, you must go the way of Scripture instead of the way of a church." More than ever I saw that biblical Christianity is a personal walk with Jesus as Lord and Saviour, not a keeping of the laws as prescribed by Mrs. White and the church hierarchy.

My last sermon in the Adventist church came from Hebrews 1:3—"Who being the brightness of his glory, and the express image of his person, and upholding all things by the word of his power, when he had by himself purged our sins, sat down on the right hand of the Majesty on high." These words had brought me solace and comfort as I prepared my last message there. At the very end of the worship hour, I told my people that our resignation from the church and denomination was effective as of that day and that there was no turning back. The announcement came as a shock, for all but a few people supported and accepted my ministry. One of the conference leaders, one we admired, was in the congregation that day, and he was dumbfounded by my resignation. The tears and confusion, even the bitterness toward the conference leaders, was obvious to everyone. Not all Adventists are convinced that Mrs. White was a genuine prophet. If one is not a leader in the church, he could get away with holding such views, but a pastor or teacher could not.

Even at this writing, my Adventist friends are heading toward a denominational split. Brave young pastors and some older theologians are saying, "We've been wrong! We've been wrong about our being a remnant church. We were wrong about the 1844 predictions. Since then, many dates and prophecies have been made but none of them have been fulfilled. We've been wrong about Mrs. White's being a true prophet." But there are those, especially among the top leadership, who are not going to give an inch until they have to; this, despite the realization of many Adventists that they have been wrong. Whether it is stubbornness, pride, or fear of losing their positions, I cannot say.*

Ruth and I received many letters and phone calls that comforted us during those trying days. Some visited us and gave us words of encouragement, and we were deeply

---

*More information on Seventh-day Adventism is contained in Appendix C found at the back of this book.

touched. But we leaned on God and thanked Him, too, for we knew that His Word had gone forth and would "not return unto [Him] void, but [would] . . . prosper in the thing whereto [God] sent it" (Isaiah 55:11).

It was only human for us to ask, "Where do we go from here? How will we live?" We had bought a home when I first took the pastorate in Tujunga. The payments and the utilities were high, and the immediate future seemed grim. Still, despite our fears, we knew that the Lord was leading us and that somehow He would provide.

The next day I dropped my letter of resignation in the mail. I have never regretted it.

I seemed a terrible failure. For the second time I had left a church where I had spent years. I was frightened, but there was never a moment when I considered forsaking the gospel ministry. By His grace, I would preach His Word wherever the door is open.

Perhaps we would have been even more frightened than we were had we realized what was ahead, for He still had some lessons to teach us so that we might be more useful vessels for His work.

12 The Learning Days

After I resigned from the Seventh-day Adventist denomination, I accepted the temporary pastorate of a small church. Ruth took several jobs as a cleaning woman for well-to-do families, but the reality of finances hit us hard as expenses outdistanced income week after week.

One day Ruth was standing at the kitchen sink washing dishes, crying softly and occasionally running her arm across her eyes to catch the tears. My mother and I were sitting at the dining room table, where I was trying to repair a toy for our three-year-old son, Steve.

I knew what was wrong, for my heart was heavy too. Not knowing what else to do, I tiptoed in and put my arm around her. She turned to me, her hands still dripping dishwater. "Oh Bart, what are we going to do? We've tried so hard, but nobody seems to care. We're short of everything, and to make matters worse, Mrs. Johnson phoned and said they're going on a month's vacation, so she won't be needing me until she gets back. I just don't know what we're going to do."

We put our house up for sale, hoping to make a few dollars. The real estate man came a few days later and told us he had an offer that was exactly what the house had cost us. He advised us to take it. So we lost our equity and didn't make a dollar.

A few weeks later I was invited to visit Richmond, California, for an interview with the pulpit committee of the local Church of God. I had little knowledge of the Church of God denomination, but after the interview, both they and I felt that I could meet their need; so we moved, and I became pastor of the Vista Hills Community Church in the Bay Area near San Francisco.

It was a small church, there being only eighteen people present at my first service, but the church had a large day-care center, and we thought that there was excellent potential for growth. Ruth and I resolved to have the church full by Easter, three months hence. We did lots of advertising, initiated new programs for the community, and had more than a hundred present on Easter. However, it was evident from the first that a great cloud of spiritual apathy enveloped the church and the Richmond area. The church was located in a depressed area with many social problems, much unemployment, and a very high crime rate. There was little to occupy the time or attention of the young people, and the results were predictable.

During the 1970s a very serious problem affected the entire Bay Area, endangering the safety and security of everyone. A wave of immorality and corruption engulfed San Francisco, Berkeley, Richmond, and parts of Oakland. Martin Luther once remarked that Rome was built over Hell. If he were alive, he would have said the same thing about the Bay Area. Parts of it were like Corinth of old, or like Sodom and Gomorrah. It seemed to be drawing bad elements of society like a magnet: adulterers, homosexuals, drug addicts, thieves, rioters, and radical revolutionaries. It was dangerous to be on the street in broad daylight; on several occasions when someone was mugged on a busy street in the sight of others, no one would help.

Those were the days when the "Jesus Movement" came on the scene. The Vista Hills Community Church was somewhat caught up in this movement, so we decided to open a coffeehouse on Friday nights. In order to attract restless crowds from the streets and maintain some discipline, we took on a student from a local Bible college as youth director. With his long, flaming red hair, he was a success. Every Friday evening the sanctuary was converted into a mod atmosphere with bright colors, low lights, mismatched tables and chairs, and "gospel" records playing bouncy, rhythmic music. Wayward people of all ages were approached on the street and invited to come and "rap" with our members about any subject that interested them; then our counselors would witness to them about Jesus.

Vista Hills Community Church was becoming well known, but it was also becoming a fool's paradise, and I determined to do something about it. The coffeehouse idea wasn't winning many souls to Christ. One member complained that I used the name of Jesus too often in my preaching. Another said that my messages were too long. Some asked me not to quote so much Scripture. Another group complained that the sanctuary looked too ecclesiastical; he demanded that I do away with much of the formality of worship, dispense with the choir robes, move out of the pulpit, and "rap" with the congregation from the floor of the sanctuary.

For a while I tried to please them, but the more I did, the more they demanded. I realized that they were determined to dismantle the sanctuary and turn it into a social hall rather than a sanctified edifice wherein God's Word was preached to lift them up. They wanted to drag the church down to their level; when I disagreed, they became argumentative, angry, and insolent. Many of them went out of their way to show that they had no esteem for those who labor in the Word.

At this time a new and lively young couple joined the church. Somehow they learned that I had had a "Pentecostal" experience. They asked me, "Why don't you tell the congregation about it? This church would be more spiritual if you did. It needs fire! It needs power! The Pentecostal experience would make it come alive!"

There was no doubt that the church needed a spiritual lift, so I decided to look into the charismatic movement, which was beginning to sweep the country. In order to understand more about it, I attended a seminar on the Holy Spirit at Holy Names College, a Roman Catholic school, where Protestant and Catholic leaders met "in a spirit of brotherly love" to talk about the gifts of the Spirit, including speaking in tongues and prophesying.

At the seminar we were told that "the Holy Spirit makes the difference between a dead and a living church. It doesn't divide people but unites them, regardless of their denominational differences." Doctrines were played down as being of little or no importance when the Holy Spirit is present.

In the closing hours of the seminar, all of us gathered in a large room, where many raised their hands and began to speak in tongues and prophesy. I bowed my head and said nothing. Then, much to my surprise, I felt hands resting on my shoulders; a kind, paternal voice said, "God is calling you into work like mine." Shocked by this so-called prophecy, I opened my eyes and saw that the speaker was David du Plessis, the widely known charismatic leader. A Catholic bishop sitting next to me took my arm and said, "Let's go outside." When we had left the room, he said, "Did you hear that? Oh, what a revelation from God!" I was in a daze and couldn't say a word.

I went back to my church wonderfully disturbed, anxious to learn everything about the Holy Spirit. I had witnessed demonstrations of glossalalia (speaking in tongues) and prophesying. I wondered if I had been neglecting a vital aspect of the gospel ministry. Now I wanted to know whether the Spirit could energize my church and heal its wounds.

In a far greater sense, however, I was disturbed by the claims of charismatic and ecumenical leaders that through the ministry of the Spirit men and women of widely disparate beliefs are suddenly reconciled to each other under the banner of Christian love. Above all things, I didn't want to go against the will of God for my church or my own life; yet I was constrained to ask, "If this be true, then what shall we do with those doctrines that are clearly contrary to the Word of God? Isn't the Bible our source of truth? Will the Catholic church, the Mormon, the Adventist, and others change and become apostolic once again? Can the leopard change his spots?" I knew that deceptions are not limited to the Roman Catholic church, for many liberal churches preach dogma that lead people from the truth, and such are a reproach to God.

I knew that the Holy Spirit does not operate alone. The

Trinity—the Father, the Son, and the Holy Spirit—is not a house divided against itself. Therefore, it is heresy to say that the Holy Spirit reconciles all differences and all departures from the Word of Truth.

I saw then that a careful examination of the ecumenical and charismatic movements is of greatest importance if we are to know what they mean, how genuine they are, and where they may lead. I wanted to know the key: are the ecumenical and charismatic movements heralding the truth?

13 The Charismatics and the Ecumenical Movement

In a room off the sanctuary of a church in Van Nuys, California, a group of about fifteen believers assembled one evening to seek the "baptism of the Holy Spirit." The pastor read:

> *He [Paul] said unto them, Have ye received the Holy Ghost since ye believed? And they said unto him, We have not so much as heard whether there be any Holy Ghost. . . . And when Paul had laid his hands upon them, the Holy Ghost came on them; and they spake with tongues, and prophesied.*

Having heard these words, everyone knelt at the altar in prayer and petition. To reduce distractions, the lights were lowered and the doors were closed. Soon there arose a soft murmuring, a sound like the sighing of wind in the trees; then it rolled in waves, sometimes like a song, sometimes in pleas mingled with laughter and tears.

Several persons, claiming that they had spoken in "unknown tongues" before, acted as spiritual coaches. They moved quietly among the seekers, especially those who seemed to hesitate, urging them, "Let your tongue go." The supplicants were encouraged to repeat edifying phrases such as "Glory to God," or "Hallelujah," over and over, ever faster and faster until their tongues were loosened or confused. Some who were deeply moved, appearing to be in a trance, were eased back to lie on the floor, eyes closed. Pillows were brought for their heads as they continued in supplication for "tongues."

After a period, the sounds changed from a low murmuring to a gentle commotion. One by one, then by twos, they began uttering babbling sounds. Then several began to speak in words and phrases that no one understood, some for a few minutes, some for longer periods. No one present seemed to have understood a word. Then it was over. Everyone stood up amidst an outpouring of sincere Christian fellowship, as if loving brothers had assembled for the happiest of occasions.

I also had the experience of speaking ecstatically at this time, although in my case it was neither dramatic nor particularly impressive, even to me. It was quiet and brief. When I arose from the altar, I took a seat nearby to witness the scene, and I must confess that I was amazed. I could not help asking, "Is this a second baptism? Or is it a mere religious notion, a deep emotional experience of praise?"

During the next several months I studied and pondered whether the ecstatic utterances were a fulfillment of prophecy for this day or merely emotional expressions of joy. I read of the many wonderful gifts conferred on the early church at Corinth and elsewhere. I knew, too, that the fledgling churches that were founded during the first ten years after Christ's ascension were weak in faith, having little under-standing. The New Testament had not yet been written, and the new Christians were surrounded by a sea of idolaters and enemies. So I asked, "Is speaking in tongues now an essential sign of the Holy Spirit's presence in one's life? Is it a second baptism for today? Are such utterances a comprehensible language today? How shall we know?"

My concern went far beyond what I had seen or experienced in Van Nuys, for I observed that a worldwide controversy is swirling around both the charismatic and the ecumenical movement, both in Protestant denominations and in the Roman Catholic church.

The controversy is centered on two questions. First, does the Holy Spirit enter into a believing Christian's life as a "separate baptism" after he has received Christ into his life?

Second, is His presence evidenced today by the speaking in tongues, as it was at Pentecost? In other words, can one have the infilling of the Holy Spirit without the sign of speaking in tongues?

The questions are more than mere musings. They are among the most significant religious questions of the twentieth century, because the charismatic movement is being used worldwide by the leaders of the ecumenical movement for what are questionable purposes, to say the least. The two movements have been channeled into the same furrow. Why? Because many charismatics and ecumenical leaders claim that through the Holy Spirit the differences between denominations disappear and become meaningless. The present ecumenical movement toward a super one-world church is gaining tremendous momentum from the charismatic movement. And as we shall see, the so-called inspired teachings of charismatics are being cited as "revelations from God" to support the super one-world church.

The teaching that the Holy Spirit dispels doctrinal differences between Protestants and Catholics, or Mormons and Methodists, or Christian Scientists and Baptists, is simply contrary to Scripture. It is like saying that the Holy Spirit bridges the gap between false teachings and Scripture. Today there are many liberal Protestant churches that deny the deity of Christ and His virgin birth. Some churches, such as the Mormon, the Christian Scientist, and the Adventist, have turned to wholly unscriptural books of their own, which they claim are equal or superior to the Bible. But the Bible says, "Neither is there salvation in any other: for there is none other name under heaven given among men, whereby we must be saved" (Acts 4:12). The Apostle Paul was speaking of Jesus Christ! And God has declared that He will make war on "the great whore"(Revelation 17:1), the world church that sits on a throne with the world government of the last days.

Now, we know that the miracle of speaking in tongues did occur at Pentecost; the Bible says so. But is this same miracle valid for today? Or did it have a specific time and a specific purpose in the biblical account?

Let us look again at the scene as it was at Pentecost. Jesus had been crucified only a few weeks before. His friends and disciples had hidden for fear of their lives. The spark of life for the new church was very faint, nor did it seem possible that the teachings of Jesus of Nazareth would become a spreading flame, the hope of all the ages! But Jesus had promised "another Comforter, that he may abide with you forever; Even the Spirit of truth" (John 14:16-17). The miracle came, and to this day the Holy Spirit comes to abide with us when we are saved.

Yes, I believe in miracles. They have been sent from the hand of God for ages past and even today, but they occurred only when they were needed, and they are not likely to be repeated in these days, for they are not now needed.

Today the Holy Spirit baptizes the believer when he receives Christ as his Lord and Saviour. It is the Holy Spirit Who convicts men of sin and their need for salvation. He who believes and receives Christ becomes "the temple of the Holy Ghost" (I Corinthians 6:19), and He abides with the believer forever. He guides the believer "into all truth" (John 16:13). But we must not tempt the Holy Spirit; we must not tempt God. Some charismatics have made bold prophecies, and some have claimed miracles that are manifestly false. In so doing they tempt God.

Perhaps some of the most dramatic examples of those who tempt God are those well-meaning but misled Pentecostals who handle rattlesnakes as part of their worship. A considerable number of them have been bitten and have died, even though Jesus said, "They shall take up serpents; and if they drink any deadly thing, it shall not hurt them" (Mark 16:18). They have forgotten that it is also written, "Thou shalt not tempt the Lord thy God" (Matthew 4:7).

We know that in all spiritual things we must be wise in our judgments. We judge by the fruits that are produced. "Do men gather grapes of thorns, or figs of thistles? Even so every good tree bringeth forth good fruit; but a corrupt tree bringeth forth evil fruit" (Matthew 7:16-17).

Let us, therefore, examine some of the fruits of today's charismatic movement. Are they good? What of the personal relationships and declarations among the charismatics? What about the charismatic movement's role in the worldwide ecumenical movement?

I believe that many charismatics are making grievous, harmful errors and that many sincere people among them are being used unwittingly by others for purposes that are not to the glory of God.

It has been my lot to observe numerous abuses by charismatics who claim to have received revelations from God. Some act as if they have a private telephone line to God or as if He speaks to them through a private angel at their side. They may act as if their experiences have made them instant divine judges and authorities on both spiritual and worldly matters. Oftentimes they speak with great authority, even though they have only a little knowledge of Scripture or the history of the church. I have observed that some who say that they have received a second baptism and spoken in tongues use very poor judgment and fail to see the consequences of their words and deeds as they make prophecies. Sometimes they will allow their minds to "free-wheel," condemning others and claiming that they are revealing God's judgments. If anyone disagrees with them, they answer, "I know what happened to me. I am right! Nothing will change me! God told me."

In some instances such declarations have had tragic consequences. One devout Christian woman recently told me about a phone call she received from the charismatic leader of a "television church." The caller told her, "God told me to tell you that you are to send one hundred dollars to the church this week; if you fail, you will be afflicted with a cancer within six weeks!" Needless to say, the woman was terrified. She had to be told that the caller's demand was not only contrary to Scripture but was, in fact, an effort at extortion. It was especially cruel in that the woman had no way to raise the money.

Another instance involved a Roman Catholic college professor who was depressed because he and his wife had parted. He visited a Catholic charismatic prayer meeting, where he asked for help. A woman laid her hands on him and prayed like this: "O Lord, help this man. Crush him!

break him asunder! Make him helpless, and when he finds that he can do nothing, pick him up again, take the pieces and put them back together, and bring him and his wife together again!" This man was so frightened that he phoned a Christian friend three thousand miles away, crying, "Is this the way God works? I am suffering now! Isn't that enough? Do I have to be crushed? I can't take any more! I am losing my mind! Perhaps I should take my life!" He had to be told that the woman who had prayed such a prayer was both ignorant and foolish. God inclines His ear to us, but no one needs to tell Him how to answer prayer. He is a God of mercy and compassion Who will not give us more than we can bear. He is the Lord of a sound mind. This suffering man had to be told, "I suggest that you find a good fundamental church. Don't return to that charismatic meeting. Run from such fanatics! Look to the Bible, not to experience, for God's truth!"

Sometimes a charismatic's prophecy produces humorous responses, as it did when one crusty old gentleman, a widower, told a beautiful young girl, "God told me that you are going to marry me!" Her retort was quick and to the point: "Well, I've got something to say about that! That was your own mind, and you can forget it!" She was understandably not eager to obey such an unauthoritative "revelation."

The Roman Catholic church and some Protestant denominations, especially those in the World Council of Churches, have found the charismatic movement well suited to their needs for promoting a worldwide super-church. The "one brotherhood of love" sounds very reasonable and even holy. But the unity of churches that dissent from the Bible cannot be approved by God.

Jesus warned against those who misuse their gifts and fail to submit to the will of God. He said, "Not everyone that saith unto me, Lord, Lord, shall enter into the kingdom of heaven; but he that doeth the will of my Father which is in heaven. Many will say to me in that day, Lord, Lord, have we not prophesied in thy name? and in thy name have cast out devils? and in thy name done many wonderful works? And then will I profess unto them, I never knew you: depart from me, ye that work iniquity" (Matthew 7:21-23).

Today even the faithful may find it difficult at times to separate truth from error. The situation is ripe for clever men to manipulate. But one cannot go wrong when he sticks to the Word of God, rightly dividing it and judging each tree by its fruit, whether it be good or evil.

Viewing the ecumenical/charismatic compromises in this light, I became more and more apprehensive of the intrigues of religious-political leaders who seek the formation of a one-world church. Because of my opposition to the charismatic movement and my background as a Catholic priest, I felt a very strong call to leave the church at Richmond and to start a ministry to those still in bondage to Rome.

My wife and I decided to step out on faith and return to San Diego, where I had been a priest.

The Brewer family: Dr. Brewer, Steven, and Ruth.

14 A Mission to Catholics

I remember as if it were yesterday the agony of my soul and the torment in my heart as I realized from the Word of God that I, a Roman Catholic priest, was lost.

I was a child of the Roman Church, but this by no means meant that I was a child of God! I was a priest, but I was far from Him. Like millions of Catholics, I was obsessed with the trappings and traditions of the church. I believed that my hope of eternal salvation could be realized only through the church and its sacraments. Like millions of others, I believed that my sins could be forgiven only by a priest; I had been taught that the priests are instruments of salvation, even though they themselves may be the vilest of men.

I taught and believed the deception that the pope's word is equal to the Word of God; moreover, I believed that wherever the supreme pontiff's dictatorial instructions are contrary to God's Word, the pope's word is preeminent. I besought the help of Mary, the mother of Jesus, calling her my intercessor, coequal with Christ, and I believed that the saints can and do protect Catholics who venerate them and ask them to appeal our cases in Heaven.

Like all Catholic priests, I substituted ritual for faith and tradition for the Word of God. Having been trained to fit the mold, I was like one of the sanctimonious Pharisees, to whom Jesus said, "Full well ye reject the commandment of God, that ye may keep your own tradition" (Mark 7:9). I taught a pagan

Catholic doctrine that the dead must suffer purgatory for the complete expiation of sin, for I did not know the Scripture that "he is able also to save them to the uttermost that come unto God by him [Jesus], seeing he ever liveth to make intercession for them" (Hebrews 7:25).

Even as a priest I knew little of the Bible, since all Catholics, including priests, are strictly forbidden to interpret Scripture in any way other than that which Catholic prelates of the Vatican have said. I dared not claim full understanding of Scripture, no matter how clear or simple it might be. Therefore, I was a stranger to His grace and I knew not that when we accept Jesus as Lord and Saviour, our sins are forgiven, forgotten, cleansed, and gone, and that it is written, "As far as the east is from the west, so far hath he removed our transgressions from us" (Psalm 103:12).

Like others, I made commerce out of salvation.

What ecstasy and what joy were mine when I knew God's Word and saw that it is honey and milk and bread and meat for the hungry soul! What unspeakable joy was given me when I took God's Word to my heart: "For by grace are ye saved through faith; and that not of yourselves: it is the gift of God: Not of works, lest any man should boast. For we are his workmanship, created in Christ Jesus unto good works" (Ephesians 2:8-10).

Then I knew that I needed no intercessor between God and me, neither Mary nor any saint. For in God's Word we read, "We have not an high priest which cannot be touched with the feelings of our infirmities; but was in all points tempted like as we are, yet without sin. Let us therefore come boldly unto the throne of grace, that we may obtain mercy, and find grace to help in time of need" (Hebrews 4:15-16).

In God's message of salvation I found that the sacrament of penance, the repetitive sacrificing of Christ in the mass, Extreme Unction, and the doctrine of purgatory have no foundation whatsoever in Scripture. The additions of unauthorized and spurious books to the Catholic Bible are additions for deception and guile. The Roman Catholic church, rooted in the paganism of Roman caesars, is a counterfeit, designed by perfidious men, not for salvation but for a lucrative commerce in sin and its forgiveness, and the extension of the church's international political powers.

Salvation is free—man cannot earn it—and in God's plan there is no deception. He is true to His Word, "And this is the promise that he hath promised us, even eternal life" (I John 2:25). For "God hath chosen the foolish things of the world to confound the wise; and God hath chosen the weak things of the world to confound the things which are mighty" (I Corinthians 1:27).

Over and over, the Scriptures reveal Jesus as the Christ, the anointed One. "There is none other name under heaven given among men, whereby we must be saved" (Acts 4:12). Only Christ can forgive sin; no priest has any office in that. Jesus said, "I am the way, the truth, and the life: no man cometh unto the Father, but by me" (John 14:6).

Christ deputized no man on earth to take His place. How utterly ridiculous, then, it is for the Catholic church to claim that the pope can speak "infallibly" for God, while it also unblushingly admits that Hell is lined with popes, cardinals, and hosts of the faithful who died in a state of mortal sin. That makes God capricious, a pagan god who must be propitiated over and over and with whom Catholics must literally gamble for Heaven or Hell.

When I was born again, a child of the living God, my heart became aglow with a vehement desire to tell the world of His wonderful salvation. Yet I could not help grieving for the years that the locust had eaten. I yearned to cause my Catholic friends to open the Bible and read and understand it, for it is the immutable and eternal Word of God. It is the written communication of God to mankind.

It seemed impossible to me that anyone hearing the truth could remain indifferent to it. Yet, at one time I closed my eyes and ears to the truth, but there were those beloved Christian witnesses who brought light to me, and my soul was filled and my life changed completely when I drank of the living waters.

In 1973, therefore, my wife and I founded the Mission to Catholics in San Diego, California, so that we could be more effective instruments in reaching Catholic friends and winning them to Christ through ministering in churches, by radio, and through literature. We love them and understand their condition and the frustrations in their hearts.

I want everyone to realize that salvation, purchased at so costly a price on Calvary's cross, is a matter solely between God and the individual soul. It is a gift, not in part, but the whole. Christ died once for us. As He hung on the cross, pinioned between two thieves, He cried, "It is finished!" The work of redemption was done. My salvation was purchased there that day because He died in my place. But there is more! He arose from the grave! He is "the firstfruits of them that slept" (I Corinthians 15:20). He gained glorious and eternal victory over death and spiritual destruction for you and for me, and He ascended into heaven, where He lives now and forevermore. One day many shall stand before His Great White Throne to receive judgment. But not all. The soul who has received Him as Lord and Saviour "shall not come into condemnation; but is passed from death unto life" because he is born again, a child of God, an heir, to share in the glory of His presence for ever and ever (John 5:24).

Many times I have been asked why I did not remain in the Roman Catholic church and work for reforms from within. We are often criticized because we are not more benign in our attitude toward the Catholic church. We are asked to be "more constructive."

But we cannot and dare not. Can the incredibly rich empire that replaced that of the Roman caesars be reformed? Martin Luther initially tried to end the corrupt practice of selling indulgences, but he failed to win Catholic reformation, even though he used nothing other than Scripture to uphold his teachings, and even today he is labeled a heretic, an enemy of God! The Catholic church never hesitates to place its condemnation on anyone who points out its false teachings or who exposes the wrongs of its leaders. Thus it tries to frighten into submission any who would reveal its deceptions.

Yes, many have worked for reform from within, but the hierarchy of the church will not listen, nor can it afford to.

Can new wine be put into old skin bottles? Can the leopard change its spots? Will the pope give up his triple tiara? No. For if the Catholic church truly conformed itself to the spirit and the teachings of Christ, there would be a complete change, not only in the Catholic church but throughout the world! None would be called "father," nor would any man claim that he is able to forgive sin; and all the dictates of the church which are contrary to the Word of God would disappear in a cleansing flood.

The Apostle Paul prophesied the incredible apostasy of the Catholic church: "For I know this, that after my departing shall grievous wolves enter in among you, not sparing the flock" (Acts 20:29). He saw the dangers of false shepherds leading the descent into perdition.

We have found this new ministry a joyous work, for we are kept by the power of God through faith. I have been reviled and physically assaulted. Nor have my wife and son been spared persecution. We have received bitter denunciations with packages of ashes containing letters of hate saying, "This will be your fate."

In times of heaviness we read again the words of the Apostle Peter: "That the trial of your faith, being much more precious than of gold that perisheth, though it be tried with fire, might be found unto praise and honour and glory at the appearing of Jesus Christ: Whom having not seen, ye love; in whom, though now ye see him not, yet believing, ye rejoice with joy unspeakable and full of glory" (1 Peter 1:7-8).

"For I am not ashamed of the gospel of Christ: for it is the power of God unto salvation to everyone that believeth; to the Jew first, and also to the Greek [Gentile]. For therein is the righteousness of God revealed from faith to faith: as it is written, The just shall live by faith" (Romans 1:16-17).

Note: The address of Mission to Catholics International, Inc. is P.O. Box 19280, San Diego, CA 92119.

Appendix A
What the Church Doesn't Want You to Know About History

When the Son of God walked the earth, He traveled with a band of twelve disciples, whom He trained for the greatest work in history. To them He said, "I will build my church" (Matthew 16:18). Later, just before His ascension, He gave them much of the responsibility for furthering His work: "Ye shall be witnesses unto me . . . unto the uttermost part of the earth" (Acts 1:8). Ten days later, from His place at the right hand of the Father, Christ sent the Holy Spirit to empower the disciples for their work.

Almost immediately the infant church met with persecution. Peter and John were arrested for preaching in the temple area (Acts 4:1); Stephen, a man "full of the Holy Ghost" (Acts 6:3) was stoned to death (Acts 7:58); James was executed by Herod (Acts 12:2). The believers were scattered throughout the Roman Empire, as seeds are blown to the corners of the earth (Acts 8:4). Satan, realizing his error in believing that the Messiah's death was God's failure (I Corinthians 2:8), sought to bleed the newborn church to death. But as the church father Tertullian noted, "The blood of the martyrs became the seed of the church"; Christ's work grew, despite the persecution.

In the year 313, after three centuries of terrible persecution of the Christians, great changes came over the Roman Empire. Constantine, a general in the Roman army, became emperor. He had gotten there by treachery and murder, and he had powerful enemies. There was even a rival claimant to the throne. Rome, corrupt beyond all telling, was sinking deeper into the abyss of depravity and greed. The empire seemed determined to destroy itself. In many large cities, hedonism characterized the day and sex orgies the nights. The home and family were breaking down; juvenile gangs roamed the streets, terrorizing the inhabitants. Agriculture was failing, and food became scarce. Unemployment often reached fifty percent. Because little was produced, the ships that had once carried great cargoes of merchandise from Italy to Africa, the Middle East, and the British Isles lay empty in the ports. Barbarians from France and Germany, finding that they could raid the countryside without fear of retaliation, wreaked havoc.

It was in this degenerate society that Constantine came to the throne of the empire. He needed help, he needed it quickly, and he was eager to get it any way he could. Looking about, he realized that the worshipers of Christ numbered in the thousands. They had established themselves wherever they went, and they proved to be honest, courageous, and forthright. When he took the matter up with his advisors, they recommended that he seek the Christians' support. So with the same shrewdness that had brought him to the throne, Constantine began wooing the Christians. He claimed that he had seen a vision and was now a Christian himself. He bestowed rich gifts on the Christian community, built churches, and elevated Christians to high positions. The Christians became the unifying factor that preserved the empire for another hundred years.

The early church paid a heavy price, however. She was ill prepared. When Emperor Theodosius the Great made Christianity the state religion in 395, thousands upon thousands of frightened pagan Romans and barbarians from outlying regions were brought into the church by baptism alone. The church was swamped, but few of the converts understood what conversion meant; even fewer knew Jesus' teachings. For most new "Christians," Christianity was simply a way to achieve better living conditions and to gain favor with the government.

As they came into the church, the "converts" brought their pagan rites and their old gods and goddesses. Pagan priests who claimed they were new Christians brought their accoutrements with only minor changes. Pagan ancestor worship became "Christian" prayers and rites for the dead. Superstitions surrounding pagan charms and amulets were replaced by veneration of relics, such as alleged pieces of the cross, bones of saints, and bits of hair or cloth. Holy days, chants, and invocations to the old pagan gods seeped into the church. An ancient pagan custom of eating and drinking the literal flesh and blood of animals and birds was still practiced by some. Many pagan gods and goddesses emerged as Catholic saints.

The Roman Empire gradually collapsed in the fifth century, after it was divided between the two sons of Emperor Theodosius. Drained by taxes, ruined by a large, incompetent, and corrupt bureaucracy, and torn by internal strife and the attacks of barbarian invaders, the empire grew so weak that it could no longer defend itself. Then Europe plunged headlong into a long night of chaos and suffering. The thin thread of civilization was nearly severed. Mankind degenerated into a state of utter despair, and Europe became a terrible and savage land. Except for a few isolated spots, stability and security vanished, and education and opportunity were only vague memories.

The church, seated in Rome, stepped into the vacuum. There was no other government or institution that could hold society together. To its credit, it must be said that the church probably saved European civilization from extinction, for only in monasteries and convents did men and women still find the time, the opportunity, and the security to study, write, paint, and preserve knowledge. The scholars and artisans of those days isolated themselves or labored under the patronage of some lord, while in most of Europe ravaging armies and bands of hungry thieves thundered throughout the land.

The Catholic church became chained by its traditions, rites, and corporate power. By the eleventh century, tradition had led the Catholic church astray like a false compass that diverts a ship from its true course. "Peter's Bark" was guided no longer solely by the Word of God, but by a committee called the College of Cardinals. Pagan rites, some dating from as far back as the Babylonian Empire, were adopted as sacred doctrines. It was taught that the mass is a reenactment of Calvary, that the pope is supreme, that St. Peter was the first pope, and that there must be a sharp separation between the clergy and the laity. Many new doctrines were added to the Bible: belief in purgatory, adoration of Mary and the saints, confession to a priest, priestly authority to forgive sin, and the persecution of heretics. Faith in Jesus Christ, as taught by the Scriptures, was corrupted for millions, being replaced by trust in the pope, the sacraments, and a growing body of traditions.

Many devout and learned men loudly condemned the church's departure from Scripture. But the powerful hierarchy tolerated no criticism. Its critics were condemned as revolutionaries and branded as heretics. It was the old Roman Empire all over again, but this time under the sign of the cross.

At the end of the eleventh century, the church had reached a pinnacle of power. Under Pope Gregory VII (1073-1085), the church was Europe's chief landlord. In some countries, it owned more than sixty percent of the arable land. Bishops and priests were often powerful magistrates. The church set up and deposed kings and princes. It placed an annual tax ("Peter's pence") on every household in England, Denmark, Sweden, Norway, Iceland, Hungary, and Poland. The church was rich, but it was also very cruel and corrupt. Immorality by popes and clergy was rampant.

In the meantime, western Europe was beginning to emerge from its seven centuries of darkness. It was on the move, curious, hungry, and as eager for trouble as a great bear awakened from a long winter's sleep. Feudal knights, often the scions of rich families, pranced about Europe looking for excitement, romance, and trouble. Armies were formed, and wars were inevitable.

The church tried to turn Europe's restlessness to its own advantage. Under its banners, crusading armies were raised to drive the Muslims out of the Holy Lands and to find the Holy Grail—the cup (or platter) used by Jesus at the Last Supper. In those days many of the crusaders hardly knew where they were going or why they were fighting; except for the princes and knights who led them, they were simple, illiterate folk from the farms, villages, and streets of Europe. The pope promised them loot, adventure, and eternal bliss in Heaven if they killed Muslims or other heretics. Hordes of ignorant men, sometimes numbering hundreds of thousands, headed east, hardly knowing where they were going. They fought and died, looted and ravaged. Eight times this happened during the eleventh, twelfth, and thirteenth centuries.

Pope Innocent III initiated the Fourth Crusade in 1202 for the purpose of driving the Muslims from Palestine and uniting the eastern and western churches. The crusaders marched, often ravaging the countryside, and finally reached eastern Europe, where, finding the Muslims too powerful and warlike, they abandoned the crusade. The city of Venice, Italy, was very angry about this, however, for its people had paid the crusaders' transportation. They had expected to make a great profit when the crusaders had finished their destruction and driven out the Muslims. The bankers wanted their money back. The crusaders were persuaded to attack and loot the city of Zara (now in Yugoslavia), because it was a rival to Venice in the maritime trade, and Venice wanted no competition. The crusaders all but destroyed Zara; they showed themselves to be so cruel that the pope excommunicated them, though he later forgave them.

In 1204 the crusaders attacked and looted Constantinople (now Istanbul, Turkey). For three days they plundered and sacked the great city, stealing or destroying all but a small part set aside for the clergy. Especially coveted were religious relics, which the crusaders spread throughout Europe.

There were even two "children's crusades." One, which began in France about 1212, is said to have involved about thirty thousand unarmed boys and girls who, with encouragement of the church, sailed for the Holy Lands from Marseilles, France, in a fleet of ships provided by slave traders. They never reached Palestine; they were taken instead to Alexandria, Egypt, where most of them were sold into slavery. Very few ever reached their homelands again. Another group of children started from Germany and undertook a march across the Alps into Italy. Thousands died of hunger or froze to death in the Alpine snows.

The crusaders brought intolerance and brutality, creating bitterness that exists until this day. There was so much tragedy that historians have never been able to sort out the full effects of the crusaders' devastations. Even now, one tragedy stands out: the Byzantine empire was wrecked (with papal approval), paving the way for the Turks to overwhelm Constantinople.

About the year 1175, the church embarked on the infamous Inquisition—the butchering and burning of "heretics" throughout Europe. Using its unlimited magisterial and religious powers, it became the total and evil dictator of Europe. It made no pretense of following the teachings of the Bible. It taxed people beyond what they could bear. It confiscated land, exacted tribute, and stole property by intrigue and extortion. Its holiness was sacrificed on the altars of greed. The story of the Inquisition is every bit as brutal and bloody as that of Hitler's murders in German and Polish concentration camps.

Pope Innocent III (1198-1216) directed the murder and robbery of more than one million people simply because they rejected papal supremacy. In 1208, he proclaimed a crusade against the Albigenses of southern France, and more than 100,000 were killed in one day. Thousands more were relentlessly pursued and killed, until by the end of the fourteenth century the Albigenses ceased to exist.

With the blessings of Pope Gregory XIII (1502-1585), ten thousand French Huguenots were slain in Paris on St. Bartholomew's Day, August 24, 1572. The news was received by the papal court with such joy that church bells were rung and a special coin was minted, bearing the words, *"Ugonottorum Strages, 1572"*—"The Slaughter of the Huguenots, 1572."

The church has even tried to rewrite history to justify

itself. To this day the history taught in monasteries, convents, and Catholic parochial schools is not the same history taught in other schools. Catholic history skips over the church's evils, seeking to make students believe that in pre-Protestant days, the spirit and teachings of Christ flowered in richness and truth. It would have students believe that the Catholic church was the government of those times and had to be stern to maintain law and order. Such teachings are false.

The church may twist some parts of history and ignore others, but it cannot destroy truth any more than a trick photographer can destroy his subject. History is not Catholic or Protestant, Greek or Roman. It is the record of the past, whether the past be good or bad. It is feared only by those who would twist it for their own purposes.

The history of the Catholic church is the history of paganism, corruption, and the lust for power. The church has not mellowed, and it should not be trusted.

Appendix B
Roman Catholic False Doctrine

During the last years I spent in the priesthood, I was learning many things about my church—things that pained and confused me. After the Second Vatican Council (1962-1965), when the church "modernized" itself, millions of devout Catholics believed that the Vatican would remove most of the opprobrious bans that had straitjacketed the church. They hoped that the vow of celibacy would be eased, birth control would be allowed, and the dictatorial doctrines related to papal infallibility would be ended. Those of us who were watching and praying hoped that the church would disavow the wrongs in its past by applying the remedy of truth. We hoped that the church would find healing and a new life inspired by the Scriptures.

However, the changes made by Vatican II were merely cosmetic. The church preferred the false teachings of Thomas Aquinas, the writings of the hateful Alphonsus Liguori, and the decrees of the Council of Trent to the gospel of Jesus Christ and the inspired writings of the apostles. Pagan tradition and rites were still given equality with the Word of God, and nothing was done that might interfere with the Vatican's riches.

Transubstantiation

There are many examples of false doctrines that required reexamination, but none more so than the doctrine of transubstantiation. Catholic doctrine teaches that the priest is endowed with power to change the bread and wine of the mass into the literal body and blood of Christ. The Roman Catholic Catechism of Christian Doctrine says, "The Holy Mass is one and the same sacrifice with that of the Cross inasmuch as Christ, who offered Himself, a bleeding victim, on the Cross to His Heavenly Father, continues to offer Himself in the unbloody manner on the altar, through the ministry of His priests."

This doctrine is nothing more than a medieval superstition deliberately foisted on the church. It was not even introduced until A. D. 1215. From the first, its purpose was to make people believe that the priest had miraculous powers and to cause them to think that they were dependent on the priest for salvation. It was nothing less than a club to beat Catholics into submission.

There is not one verse in the Bible that clearly supports the doctrine of transubstantiation. We are told to celebrate the Lord's Supper, using bread and wine as symbols of his flesh and blood, but we are not asked to be cannibals. The Bible tells us, "We are sanctified through the offering of the body of Jesus Christ once for all. . . . For by one offering he hath perfected for ever them that are sanctified" (Hebrews 10:10, 14). On the Cross He cried, "It is finished" (John 19:30).

The doctrine of transubstantiation is not only heresy; it is blasphemy!

Veneration

Another dogma that has bothered Catholics for centuries is the veneration of relics and the claims that they have magical powers. Even Martin Luther wondered how there could be twenty-six apostles buried in Germany, when there were only twelve in the entire Bible! It is said that if all the pieces of the cross displayed in Catholic churches were assembled together, it would take a ten-ton truck to carry them. It is clear that most "relics" are frauds. Furthermore, there is nothing in the Bible that supports the veneration of relics, even if they are genuine.

The same is true of images in the church, such as Stations

of the Cross. The church claims that they are not "images" because they represent people who actually lived, but the second commandment reads, "Thou shalt not make unto thee any graven image, or any likeness of any thing that is in heaven above, or that is in the earth beneath, or that is in the water under the earth" (Exodus 20:4). Can anyone deny that statues of the apostles and other saints are images? If they are not venerated as images, why are candles burned before them? Why are they often garlanded with flowers? Why do priests and laity bow and pray before them? Why are such images carried aloft on thrones during celebrations? The Hindus of India are condemned as idolaters because they carry their idols in similar celebrations during their annual festival of light. Are such things right for Catholics but wrong for Hindus? The Bible clearly condemns all images, for it is written, "I am the Lord: that is my name: and my glory will I not give to another, neither my praise to graven images" (Isaiah 42:8).

My questioning of the veneration of images led me to question the veneration of the Virgin Mary, also called "the Mother of God," "the Queen of Heaven," "the Door to Paradise," and "the Sorrowful Mother."

Assuredly the Virgin Mary was a special woman, chosen of God. When she was carrying Jesus in her womb, she sang, "My soul doth magnify the Lord, and my spirit hath rejoiced in God my Saviour. For he hath regarded the low estate of his handmaiden: for, behold, from henceforth all generations shall call me blessed" (Luke 1:46-48).

Yes, she is "blessed." But there is not one verse in the Bible that elevates her to divinity as the Queen of Heaven or as an intercessor between Christ and the Christian. In fact, the Bible teaches quite the contrary. Mary, too, claimed God as her Saviour (Luke 1:47); she, too, was a sinner. There was once a woman who said to Jesus, "Blessed is the womb that bare thee, and the paps which thou hast sucked." Jesus replied, "Yea rather, blessed are they that hear the word of God, and keep it" (Luke 11:27-28). Jesus once asked a rhetorical question of his followers: "Who is my mother? and who are my brethren?" Then he answered his own question:

"Whosoever shall do the will of my Father which is in heaven, the same is my brother, and sister, and mother" (Matthew 12:48, 50).

Is Mary an intercessor? No, our intercessor is Christ. "We have an advocate with the Father, Jesus Christ the righteous: And he is the propitiation for our sins: and not for our's only, but also for the sins of the whole world" (I John 2:1-2). "There is one God, and one mediator between God and men, the man Christ Jesus" (I Timothy 2:5).

The Papacy

The entire Catholic church is built on the assumption that Christ appointed Peter the first pope and thereby established the papacy. But was St. Peter the first pope? Is the pope truly his successor? Does the pope have authority in faith and morals over every pastor and his flock?

I found that the answer to each of these questions is a resounding "No!"

Romanists quote Matthew 16:15-18 and then add their own interpretation to establish their claim that the Roman bishop is St. Peter's successor, supreme and infallible. That Scripture reads: "He saith unto them, But whom say ye that I am? And Simon Peter answered and said, Thou art the Christ, the Son of the living God. And Jesus answered and said unto him, Blessed art thou, Simon Bar-jona: for flesh and blood hath not revealed it unto thee, but my Father which is in heaven. And I say also unto thee, That thou art Peter [*petros*], and upon this rock [*petra*] I will build my church; and the gates of hell shall not prevail against it."

Was the church built on Peter? No, it was built on Peter's confession, "Thou art the Christ, the Son of the living God." Speaking to Peter, Jesus used the word *petros*—a masculine noun meaning "pebble." He used the word *petra*—a feminine word which means "rock"—in speaking of the foundation of His church. It was Peter's confession on which the church would be built.

There is no verse in the Bible in which Christ conferred any more authority on Peter than he did any other apostle or even the apostles' co-workers. If Christ had wanted to establish Peter as the supreme head of the church, would he not have said, "Now, when I ascend to My Father which is in Heaven, I want you all to obey Peter, for I am appointing him as My vicar on earth"? But Jesus was silent on this point; he made no special mention of Peter.

It is quite clear from Peter's own writings that he never thought of himself as supreme head of the church. Even the Apostle Paul on one occasion criticized Peter: "I withstood him to the face, because he was to be blamed" (Galatians 2:11).

The Vatican claims that St. Peter was the first pope, yet it cannot prove that there was any pope, with the power it claims for the papacy, before the sixth century. The first Roman bishop who took the title of pope was Boniface III in A. D. 607. Even the great St. Augustine, bishop of Hippo, refused to recognize the bishop in Rome as his superior. He wrote, "Whoever wants to appeal to those beyond the sea [i.e., in Rome] shall not be received by anyone in Africa to the communion."

There was great rivalry during the first four centuries for supremacy among the bishops of Rome, Constantinople, Carthage, and Antioch. The reason the bishop of Rome finally gained supremacy was the power of the city of Rome itself, not the spiritual or temporal authority of the Roman bishop. Rome was the world's greatest center of communication, learning, writing, and transportation. Thus the Roman bishop gained more attention than other bishops—eventually enough to establish supremacy. Even the Catholic church is unable to show one decree, canon, or resolution by any ecumenical council during the first six hundred years after Christ that gives any spiritual supremacy to the bishop of Rome. The papacy's rise to power was purely political.

The claim that the popes are or have been infallible is utterly ridiculous. Such claims are proved false even by the *Catholic Encyclopedia*. Many popes have been grossly immoral; some have been murderers and adulterers, and the papal office has been sold more than once. Popes have contradicted themselves as well as previous popes. Adrian II (867-872) declared civil marriages valid, but Pope Pius VII

(1800-1823) condemned them. Sixtus V (1585-1590) recommended reading the Bible; Pius VII condemned it. Popes have been guilty of heresy even by Catholic definitions. Honorius I (625-638) held to monotheism, a belief condemned as heretical by his successor, Severinus.

Purgatory

Yet another key Catholic doctrine, that of purgatory, is not mentioned or even implied by any verse in the entire Bible. In fact, the Bible completely contradicts the very concept of purgatory. "For by grace are ye saved through faith; and that not of yourselves: it is the gift of God: Not of works, lest any man should boast" (Ephesians 2:8). The Apostle Paul writes, "There is therefore now no condemnation to them which are in Christ Jesus" (Romans 8:1). There is no place of suffering for those saved ones who have died.

Then where are the dead?

Our human bodies are "fearfully and wonderfully made" (Psalm 139:14), but they are mortal. They are made from the chemicals of the earth, for as the Bible says, "In the sweat of thy face shalt thou eat bread, till thou return unto the ground; for out of it wast thou taken: for dust thou art, and unto dust shalt thou return" (Genesis 3:19). Man's spirit, however, does not go into the earth, nor does it die; for our eternal God "breathed into [man's] nostrils the breath of life; and man became a living soul" (Genesis 2:7). Man's soul is the very breath of God.

When the soul of a child of God departs its earthly temple, it goes to be with the Lord, awaiting the day of resurrection. The Bible says, "Then shall the dust return to the earth as it was: and the spirit shall return unto God who gave it" (Ecclesiastes 12:7). Death is a change of residence for the soul. As William Booth, the founder of the Salvation Army, said, "Death is a promotion to glory for His children."

Purgatory is a mere invention of man, having its origin in the idolatrous religious practices of ancient Babylon, Egypt, and Greece. Why, then, has the church accepted the doctrine? As one Catholic priest put it, "Purgatory is the Klondike of the Roman Catholic church." It is an inexhaustible gold mine yielding vast treasure from those who are tormented with the belief that dead parents, children, or other loved ones are suffering in purgatory to be purged of their sins. What needless pain and suffering some Catholics bear! How many millions spend their money for masses for the dead! Yet they spend it for nothing. And as if this were not enough, Catholic theologians have added spurs to the fears of devout Catholics by dredging up the imagined horrors of purgatory. Thomas Aquinas, great "doctor of the church," wrote, "Nothing but the eternal duration makes the fire of Hell more terrible than that of purgatory." Yet the Apostle Paul wrote, "We are confident, I say, and willing rather to be absent from the body, and to be present with the Lord" (II Corinthians 5:8).

The Apocrypha

One last question concerning the doctrines of the Catholic church is common: "Why does the Catholic Bible differ from the Protestant Bible? Why does it contain books not found in the Protestant Bible?" There is a reason.

There are seven books that the Roman Catholic church adds to the Old Testament. They must be accepted as Scripture by every Roman Catholic, under peril of mortal sin.

These books, known as the apocrypha, are:
1. Tobit
2. Judith
3. The Wisdom of Solomon
4. Ecclesiasticus, or The Wisdom of Jesus, the Son of Sirach
5. Baruch
6. I Maccabees
7. II Maccabees

The apocrypha are not canonical. They are not accepted by the Jews, because they are either spurious or of unknown origin. They conflict with history, geography, and theology. The New Testament quotes three hundred times from the Old Testament, but not once from an apocryphal book.

Josephus, the noted Jewish historian, and other learned men of the first century after Christ prepared a list of the books of the Jewish law and prophets, but their list contained none of the apocryphal books. St. Jerome, the fifth-century scholar and translator recognized by the Catholic church as one of its greatest doctors, emphatically denied that the apocrypha forms any part of the Old Testament. It has been noted that "even in the papacy, the Apocrypha was not considered canonical until the Council of Trent added it to the Old Testament and pronounced it so." The council "canonized" the apocryphal books because some of them contain verses referring to such things as prayers for the dead, which Rome has found useful.

The key doctrines of the Roman church are without foundation. The Roman system has been built up over the years in an effort to keep its people in bondage. I once knew the agony of that bondage. I have written these things not in anger, but so that others might be encouraged to search the Scriptures. There they will find the truth, the hammer that will break their chains and free their souls.

Appendix C
The Early Days of Ellen G. White and Seventh-day Adventism

Ellen Gould Harmon was born on November 26, 1827, to Robert and Eunice Harmon in the little town of Gorham, Maine. Her family was of modest means, her father being a garment maker. Apparently she was sickly from birth and became a victim of a respiratory disease at an early age. Her health was so precarious that several doctors despaired of her living beyond adolescence. She was unable to run and romp like other children and often had to sit on the sidelines or watch from a window while the others played hide-and-seek or blind-man's bluff. Yet even though she was quiet and shy, her father observed that she was highly intelligent and gifted with an unusually vivid imagination and an inventive mind.

Children are often cruel to those less fortunate than they, and it was so in Ellen's case. One day when she was nine years old, a girl picked up a large stone and hurled it at her, hitting her in the face, breaking her nose, and permanently disfiguring her. For days she lay in a coma, hovering between life and death. When she regained consciousness, she was afflicted with nervous disorders that remained with her for the rest of her life.

She began to have strange seizures, usually without warning. She would fall unconscious to the floor, suddenly but temporarily losing all feeling. Her body would become still and rigid; her heart would race and beat irregularly. Frequently during these spells, she appeared to be near death.

She described her own condition: "My health failed rapidly. I could only talk [sic] in a whisper or broken tone of voice. I would awake with my mouth full of blood." Medical doctors who are specialists in the treatment of nervous disorders have diagnosed her condition as a type of hysteria or catalepsy.

Her father, who loved her very much, made every effort to provide some kind of schooling for her, and as a final effort he enrolled her in a girl's school where she could receive special attention. Her trembling was so severe, however, that she could not hold a pencil or write on a slate. The school sent her home.

In 1841, at the age of thirteen, she was taken to a camp meeting to hear an itinerant preacher named William Miller, a farmer from Pittsfield, Massachusetts, and a former army captain in the War of 1812. He had become widely known for his mighty sermons and awesome predictions. Since 1840 he had traveled throughout New England, preaching that Jesus Christ would come back to earth in 1843. He declared that as he studied Daniel 8 and 9, God revealed to him the time of the Advent, or Second Coming, of Jesus Christ. By reasoning and arithmetic, he concluded that the secret of Daniel's vision was a 2300-year period between the end of "the captivity of the Jews in Babylon" and the coming of the Messiah. Miller based his mathematics on King Nebuchadnezzar's decree to rebuild Jerusalem, issued in 457 B. C. Miller added 2300 years to that date and came up with the year 1843. His predictions astounded and frightened his hearers, and he convinced so many people that great crowds attended his meetings throughout New England as he cried, "The Advent is at hand!"

Miller's predictions tied in perfectly with the spirit of the times. Feelings were rife that the last days were at hand. After the War of 1812, there was fear everywhere. Halley's comet, with its 100-million-mile-long tail, flashed across the sky in 1834, and there were showers of meteors. People saw strange hovering lights in the heavens. There were storms, earthquakes, and fires; at sea there were hurricanes, water spouts, and tidal waves. Each happening was viewed as a portent of Christ's return. Miller, who believed that he had made a great and glorious discovery, thought it his duty to warn everyone that the Kingdom of God was at hand.

When teenager Ellen heard his sermon and prophecy, she was terrified. She saw evil everywhere; she feared that Christ would come and reject her because of her sinful ways. She thought herself damned and was often beset by long periods of depression and melancholia.

Her seizures came more often. On waking, she told of visions, vividly describing the awesome sights she had seen. In one vision she saw a long, steep path leading from the earth to the great judgment throne. Friends and relatives were on the pathway, but now and then one fell and plunged into oblivion. As she repeated the story, she sometimes named names, and the terrified relatives quickly changed their ways.

There was another vision in which she saw animals being cut to ribbons and people milling about in fear and anguish while in the background loomed the grim figure of Christ. Sometimes she heard voices that told what lay in store for those who rejected her warnings. There were other visions in which she saw acquaintances who were ill and received messages explaining how they could be healed. Over and over, when her advice was followed, sick persons regained full health so rapidly that even doctors were amazed. She advised the sick to throw away all their medicines, drink copious amounts of clear, pure water, and avoid all stimulants such as coffee, tea, tobacco, and drugs. Even the doctors began to listen to her, probably because the state of medicine in the rural areas was so poor that pure water effected more cures than many medicines. It was often said that one old grandmother was worth two physicians.

Ellen's fame spread for miles around. People referred to her as a sacred prophetess, inspired by God, and sought her advice. Even Miller was impressed.

But 1843 came and passed, and Jesus didn't come. Thousands who had waited for His coming were in sore distress; many left the Adventist movement. Miller, a disappointed man, confessed his errors while exhorting the faithful to watch and wait so that the Second Coming would not catch them unawares.

Camp meetings went on, however, as Adventist leaders tried to explain their disappointments. Then one day a member of the congregation stood up and declared that he had received a revelation from God that Jesus would return in the seventh month of the Jewish calendar in 1844. This time a definite date was fixed for the end of the world: October 21, 1844. That testimony lit a fire that burned hotter than ever before. Mr. Miller's followers set out to warn the world. They cried that this time the day was "for sure"; there could be no mistake! When October 21 came near, hundreds left the cities and went into the hills to await His coming. Businesses were closed, children were taken out of school, crops were left unharvested, property was given away, and many Millerites gathered in solemn prayer.

The long-awaited day passed without Christ's appearance. There was disappointment and sadness as people tried to piece their lives together again. Many still believed in His imminent return, but they knew that somewhere, somehow, they had made a mistake. They talked among themselves and tried to understand what had gone wrong. Miller was so disappointed that he apologized for his errors and the consternation he had caused. He gave up leadership of the movement, and in his great disappointment he became ill.

Seventeen-year-old Ellen had another vision. This time she saw the Adventists walking straight up to Heaven. She declared that the 1844 date had simply been misunderstood; what it really meant was that Christ had moved into His heavenly sanctuary in 1844 to cleanse it in preparation for completing the atonement for sin that He had begun on Calvary. Apparently she based her explanation on Daniel 8:13-14—"How long shall be the vision concerning the daily sacrifice . . .? And he said unto me, Unto two thousand and three hundred days; then shall the sanctuary be cleansed." She said that Christ's work was not yet complete; sin still had to be blotted out. Christ is working in the sanctuary making "investigative judgments" to see if professed believers are really in the faith. "When this is completed, He will return to the world. At His return, the righteous who are still living will be translated to heaven, and the righteous dead will be resurrected and taken to the same place. There they will spend the millennium—and not on the earth. The earth will be desolate during this whole period. Meanwhile, the punishment of the wicked will be determined. After this unique millennium, Christ will return to the earth with the righteous 'where eternity will be spent.' Satan and the wicked will be annihilated."[21]

She warned that Adventists must be totally obedient to the Bible, keep the Ten Commandments, and listen to her. She claimed that she had had a vision in which she was transported to Heaven and shown tablets on which the Fourth Commandment was emblazoned in a halo of light: "Remember the sabbath day, to keep it holy. . . . The seventh day is the sabbath of the Lord thy God" (Exodus 20:8,10).

Since Saturday is the seventh day of the week, Adventists keep that day, not Sunday, as their day of rest; hence the name Seventh-day Adventists. But the New Testament does not support their view. The Apostle Paul teaches that the saved are under grace, free from the condemnation of the law. Most Christians observe Sunday as the sabbath because Christ was raised from the grave on Sunday, "the first day of the week." His resurrection is the day of our liberty and justification. Paul warns us specifically, "Let no man therefore judge you in meat, or in drink, or in respect of . . . the sabbath days: Which are a shadow of things to come; but the body is of Christ" (Colossians 2:16-17).

One day, as she neared the age of eighteen, Ellen announced that her involuntary trembling would soon stop. Shortly thereafter, she fell unconscious to the floor. When she awoke, her trembling was gone and never seriously troubled her again. With tremendous vigor she began to dictate her religious thoughts to her followers and to give audiences. She stressed that peace with God promotes good health. She emphasized the therapeutic use of water, called hydrotherapy, and vigorously opposed the use of alcohol in any form or of drugs such as opium, which was sold over the

---

[21]John H. Gerstner, *The Teachings of Seventh-day Adventism* (Grand Rapids: Baker, 1960), p. 15.

counter in many drugstores and was commonly given to babies in the form of laudanum to stop their crying or to relieve colic. She disdained the use of tobacco, tea, and coffee and warned against the use of meat and animal fats, especially butter.

At the age of twenty, Ellen met and married a young minister, James White, who himself had been too sickly with lung disorders to attend school. He was an authentic genius. Although he never had had an opportunity to attend school before the age of nineteen, he completed all grades and obtained a teacher's certificate in twelve weeks! Certainly his learning was no sham; he became Ellen's editor and publisher, correcting much of her grammar and giving her writings an excellent style. With his help, Ellen White's fame spread throughout the United States, Europe, and Australia. The Seventh-day Adventist movement was on its way to becoming a worldwide religion.

Afterword

When Vatican II was convoked on October 11, 1962, the opening session was attended by more than 2400 Roman Catholic bishops and more than 40 observers from Protestant churches. More than 1100 priests presented their views during its four sessions. It was officially closed December 8, 1965.

Pope John XXIII, on ascending the throne, saw many internal and external problems confronting "Peter's Bark." He declared, "We must open the windows, let in fresh air and discover new truths." What was done, however, may have been something else.

When the history of this century is written, Vatican II may prove to have been one of the most important movements of our time. The forces it set in motion may change the course of history for the whole world well into the next century. It may yet affect the life of every man, woman, child, and church in Christendom, especially in the United States.

There were two key reasons that this council of bishops was convoked. The first is that the Vatican seeks to bring all denominations of Christianity into the Roman Catholic fold. It is a matter progressing much more rapidly than most people realize. The second reason is the Vatican's determination to become an extraordinary political power throughout the world by the end of this century.

There is a very interesting background to all this, and

while the whole truth about the Vatican is never simple, we can see the outlines of its plans and understand why and how the church expects to attain such world power.

In order to understand this, we must go back a few years to the reign of Pope Pius XII (1939-1958). He was a strong and forceful ruler, oftentimes brilliant, and occasionally given to seeing "visions," which were sometimes followed by moods of deep depression. He was almost violently anti-Communist—so much so that he issued a decree that any Roman Catholic who became a Communist was *ipso facto*—cut off from the Roman Church.

During Pope Pius' reign, there were several bitter factions among high church dignitaries in the Vatican. There was a pro-Nazi bloc as well as a loosely organized group of moderates. There was also a third faction, a liberal socialist bloc, which had the silent support of many church officials and one of the Vatican's shrewdest diplomats, Monsignor John Roncalli.

Roncalli was only a minor diplomat during World War II, but he was widely known and well liked, particularly in Eastern Europe and the Middle East. Born to poor peasant parents who eventually had twelve children, he joined the Italian army during World War I and became a sergeant. After the war he became a priest and joined the Vatican's diplomatic corps, demonstrating unusual skill in carrying out his assignments. Likeable, with an easy-going manner, Monsignor Roncalli made many friends and few enemies among the nations of Eastern Europe. At the end of World War II, he was one of the Vatican's chief intelligence agents in Turkey, where he gathered information on Russia, Turkey, the Balkan nations, and the Middle East. The times were turbulent, but Roncalli was always cool, with a down-to-earth manner that won him trust and admiration everywhere. He knew when to speak and when to remain silent. Even the Communists trusted him and said he understood them.

Back at the Vatican there were church officials who thoroughly disliked him, but he ignored them. He seemed destined to complete a quiet career as a church diplomat and Vatican administrator.

But an event in France changed everything. Shortly after Germany surrendered to the Allies, a serious problem arose among the priests in France. It was a problem that agonized the pope. It concerned hundreds of French bishops and priests who had become pro-Nazi during the war. Some of them were accused of having helped sell out France to the French and German Nazis.

After the fall of France in 1940, Marshal Petain, a hero of World War I, was made premier of France. He asked Hitler for an armistice. On June 22, 1940, the armistice was concluded; Petain became dictator of central France. He gained considerable support from Frenchmen who thought they might profit by showing loyalty to Petain. A large number of Catholic bishops and priests supported him, even though his regime, called the Vichy Government, became notorious for its collaboration with the Germans.

When the war was over, France was outraged against Petain. He was tried for treason, found guilty, and on August 15, 1945, sentenced to death. During this time General Charles De Gaulle, who had led the French resistance movement throughout the war, became premier-president. He commuted Petain's sentence to life imprisonment and had him sent to Ile d'Yew, an island off the coast of Brittany.

De Gaulle was determined to root out and try the French who had collaborated with the Nazis. He was especially anxious to try the French bishops and priests who had collaborated with the Germans in the fall of France.

Pope Pius was equally determined that they would not be brought to trial. He himself had done nothing to stop Hitler or Mussolini, and it is alleged that he frequently cooperated with both the German and Italian dictators, believing that they would win the war. Even during the holocaust and the pogroms against the Jews, he did nothing to stop the cruelties.

But when he saw that the German war machine was being crushed by the Allies, he quickly severed ties with the Germans and ardently undertook a program of wooing the Americans. He wanted to be on the winning side, whichever it might be! He had guessed wrong, and he knew that public trials would expose some of the roles he and other high church dignitaries had played during the war. He was determined to avoid this if at all possible.

In France, a large and growing faction of French socialists suddenly emerged; this, too, included a large number of Catholic bishops and priests. Both the former pro-Nazi priests and the left-leaning priests were preaching thunderous sermons and writing articles against De Gaulle, trying to depose him from his position as premier-president. The problem was growing more serious every day. French intelligence was so weak at that time that no one could say whether or not the Vatican was behind the priests' attacks on De Gaulle.

Something had to be done quickly because De Gaulle was forming tribunals throughout France to try the former pro-Nazi priests. The Vatican desperately looked around for an astute negotiator to go to France and try to work out a deal with De Gaulle. Someone remembered Monsignor John Roncalli, a friend of socialists, a man able to get along with the Nazis, and a master of intelligence operations. He was sent to France to negotiate, and he made a political bargain with De Gaulle. He would stop the socialist and pro-Nazi priests from opposing De Gaulle if De Gaulle would agree not to put the Nazi priests on trial.

De Gaulle had no choice but to back off and abandon the program of trying the treasonous clerics. He gave his word to Roncalli, who hurriedly persuaded France's socialist Catholic clergy and the former pro-Nazi priests to stop their campaign against the premier-president. Some were stubborn, but Roncalli blessed them and told them to be patient.

Roncalli had not only won a tremendous victory for the Vatican, but he had also developed a powerful following both in the Vatican and throughout the church. He became an advisor to the pope until the matter was completely closed. The pope, who was now ardently pro-American, didn't trust Roncalli, however, and Roncalli also deplored the pope's pro-American attitude. He worked behind the scenes, careful never to defy the pope, but wherever he could he showed favor toward socialists and communists. The pope soon learned of Roncalli's actions, however, and finally had enough of him. In order to get him out of the Vatican and appease the church liberals, he gave Roncalli the red hat of a cardinal and sent him to a minor post in Vienna. He expected Roncalli to attend to his duties quietly, drop out of politics, and die peacefully.

Pope Pius died first, however. Cardinals from all over the world gathered in Rome to elect a new pope. Most of the left-leaning nations favored Roncalli to be pope; so did a large number of liberal cardinals, most of whom were Italian.

At first it appeared that the majority of cardinals favored a certain Monsignor Montini for pope, but it appears that in their conclaves, the cardinals decided that the new pope should come from the college of cardinals; Montini was thus ineligible.

Who would be the new pope? At first it didn't seem that Cardinal Roncalli had a chance, but after ten ballots, the cardinals seemed unable to agree on anyone else. Roncalli seemed to be a good "compromise candidate." He was seventy-seven years of age, overweight, a heavy smoker, and not expected to live very long. Most important of all, he was an experienced Vatican administrator and a skilled diplomat. In a world freighted with troubles and uncertainty, he seemed to be an expedient choice.

Roncalli, elected on the eleventh ballot, became Pope John XXIII. He was thought of as a sort of "care-taker" pope who would serve until a more widely acceptable candidate emerged.

What a shock the Vatican was in for! The cardinals could hardly have been more wrong in thinking of the new pope as a mere caretaker. He launched a revolution in the church such as had not been seen since the Reformation. He was a zealous reactionary against the policies and practices of his predecessor, Pope Pius XII. Pope John XXIII can properly be called "the first pink pope."

Immediately after his elevation to the papacy, he made Monsignor Montini a cardinal, thereby increasing his chances of being named the next pope. Cardinal Montini and

Pope John saw eye-to-eye on many issues, both political and religious.

Pope John also made it clear to American Cardinal Spellman, a close friend of Pius XII, that he was no longer welcome in Rome. He moved to expel most of the pro-American prelates from the Vatican, replacing them with liberals.

In public, however, the new pope's warm-heartedness, easy-going manner, and strong, earthy features won him instant recognition and made him the darling of the world's press, television, and radio. Almost overnight he became popular with Catholics and non-Catholics throughout the whole world. He became a father-figure to millions.

Yet he was aggressive and very persuasive. He instituted many church reforms; he even suggested that there are similarities between the teachings of Jesus and Karl Marx. Prominent churchmen of the liberal bloc began showing special favor toward Tito of Communist Yugoslavia and Soviet Foreign Minister Gromyko; in order to identify the church with socialists, the church often depicted Jesus as a man in overalls or a factory worker. This made a great impression on the nations of Central and South America, Africa, and the Middle East.

Why was all this done? Why were socialists and communists receiving friendship and attention from the Vatican when Pope Pius had been so bitterly anti-communist? There are several reasons.

Pope John and Vatican leaders had studied the whole world and the religious, economic, and political scenes. They had studied the sway of Catholicism, Protestantism, democracy, socialism, and communism. They studied and analyzed secret intelligence estimates from all over the world, and in plain words, the Vatican concluded that communism is likely to dominate the world by the end of this century!

Almost half of the world's rapidly growing population is already dominated by or under the influence of socialism or communism. Worldwide production of food and other necessities is not increasing as fast as population. Billions of people, especially in the poor nations, are miserable and ready to explode when strong leaders appear. Communists are eager to provide that leadership.

Russia's leaders, however, are aware that flaws, cracks, and wear are showing up in the communist system and getting worse. Even after a half-century, Russia still cannot meet its basic requirements for food, clothing, housing, transportation, and services. Russian leaders do not allow daily news to be freely disseminated, nor do they allow freedom of speech or criticism of the government. They realize that something new is needed to bolster communism's sagging zeal—something that will offset their failures.

What will it be? Religion? Increased efforts to spread the doctrine of communism? War?

Many Vatican officials believe that Catholicism can be the answer to their problems. Some prelates believe that the communists need the Vatican more than the Vatican needs the communists. There are those who believe that a reconciliation with the communists is likely to occur before the end of this century. An understanding or even an alliance between the Vatican and the Kremlin is no longer unthinkable. The late Bishop Fulton J. Sheen said a few years ago, "In the future there will be but two governments in the world: Rome and Moscow."

Is America deluding itself? Yes! The search for pleasure has swept over America like a tidal wave of sin. Many young Americans define poverty as the lack of a new automobile or a stereo set. The American people are almost totally preoccupied with their own material needs.

Jesus said, "No man can enter into a strong man's house, and spoil his goods, except he will first bind the strong man; and then he will spoil his house" (Mark 3:27). Perhaps the thief has already entered our house, but we are too preoccupied with ourselves to see him.

Glossary

abbot The head of a monastic community.

absolution See *confession.*

acolyte One who helps the priest during the mass. His chief duties are to light and carry candles and to assist the priest at the altar.

Blessed Sacrament The consecrated wafer, revered as the body of Christ in the mass.

breviary A prayer book containing various parts of the Divine Office. (See *Divine Office.*) There are several different editions of breviaries.

canticle A biblical chant or prayer, excluding the Psalms. Examples include Mary's *Magnificat* (Luke 1:46-55) and Simeon's *Nunc Dimittis* (Luke 2:29-32).

cassock A long robe worn by male clergy under liturgical garb and in everyday activities.

chalice The cup that holds the wine during the mass.

chancery The administrative office of a diocese. (See *diocese.*)

chasuble A frock worn by the priest during the mass. It is worn over the cassock. (See *cassock.*)

confession The repeating of one's sins to a priest. Following confession, the priest grants absolution, or forgiveness, and assigns penance, or works intended to earn the sinner forgiveness.

confessor The one who hears confession, grants absolution, and assigns penance. He must be at least a priest.

confiteor The prayer of confession. The form of the prayer varies among the different Catholic orders.(See *Order.)*

corpus The body (of Christ).

crucifix An image of the cross, usually bearing a corpus.

diocese The area governed by a bishop.

Divine Office The public prayer formula repeated daily by priests and those studying for the priesthood. (It is also recommended, but not required, for others.) Sometimes called the Liturgy of the Hours, it consists of Psalms, hymns, and writings from the church fathers. It is organized to follow the liturgical year, with readings for every day.

elements See *Mass.*

Eucharist The sacrament of the mass, also called Holy Eucharist. (See *Mass.)*

ex cathedra Greek for "from the chair." When the pope speaks *ex cathedra* or in his official capacity, he is said to be infallible in matters of faith and morals. *Ex cathedra* pronouncements are comparatively rare.

father The title given to Catholic clergy. A father rector rules a church, college, or seminary; a father prior rules a monastery or serves second to the abbot; a father provincial rules several monasteries of one order in a single province. (See *Order.)*

flagellate To beat with a whip or rod. Monks commonly practice self-flagellation, which, says *A Catholic Dictionary,* "in moderation and for reasons of devotion is not forbidden."

genuflect To bend the knee (usually the right knee). Genuflection is accompanied by "the sign of the cross," made on the chest.

habit The official and distinctive external garment worn by members of a religious order. The term is used of both male and female apparel.

High Mass See *Mass.*

Host The wafer, also called the Sacred Host, said to be changed into the real body of Christ during the mass.

(See *Mass.)*

indulgence The cancellation of the temporal punishment for a particular sin already forgiven. In other words, the indulgence shortens the sinner's time in purgatory. It is given in exchange for various good works, including gifts to the church. The Reformation under Martin Luther began in large part because of the church's practice of selling indulgences in advance—in effect, selling the buyer permission to sin. (See *purgatory.)*

Mass The ceremony during which the elements (wafer and wine) are supposedly changed into the body and blood of Christ through the process called transubstantiation. The mass is said to be a reenactment of Calvary. The Pontifical Mass is celebrated by the pope or a bishop, with many assistants and much extra ceremony. The High Mass, or Solemn Mass, is celebrated by a priest assisted by a deacon and a subdeacon. It includes much singing and the use of incense. The Low Mass is celebrated by a priest assisted by only an acolyte, and it includes less singing and no incense. The Mass for the Dead, formerly called the Requiem Mass, omits the more "joyous" parts of the regular mass.

minor seminary A preparatory school for candidates for the priesthood, ages twelve to eighteen.

monastery A secluded religious community overseen by an abbot or a father prior. (See *father.)*

monsignor Italian for "my lord." This title is given to the higher levels of the clergy, including the pope, archbishops, cardinals, abbots, certain priests, and members of the curia, the ruling body of the church.

monstrance The vessel that holds the consecrated Host as it is viewed by the congregation during the mass. (See, *Host, Mass.)*

mortification Bodily discipline endured for the good of the soul. Prayer is a mild form of mortification. More rigorous forms include fasting, flagellation, the wearing of uncomfortable clothing (including the "hair shirt"), endurance of extremes of temperature, and similar practices. (See *flagellation.)*

novena A nine-day period of devotion.

novice One preparing to enter religious service. He is under no obligation to continue, since he has taken no vows.

novice master One in charge of the training of novices during their novitiate.

novitiate The period of a novice's probation. It usually includes one year of seclusion in a religious community such as a monastery.

order An organized group within the Catholic church. Some orders are the Trappists, the Carmelites, the Franciscans, and the Dominicans. The church would not admit it, but orders are roughly equivalent to Protestant denominations; in many cases there is vigorous and hot-tempered competition between various orders.

ordinand One about to be ordained.

penance See *confession, sacrament.*

prior See *father.*

provincial See *father.*

purificator The cloth used to wipe the chalice and other vessels after their use in the mass. (See *chalice, Mass.*)

purgatory A supposed place of punishment for those not wicked enough to go to Hell but not good enough to go to Heaven. Purgatory's fiery punishment makes one worthy to see God. Depending upon the degree of the person's wickedness, the length of stay in purgatory varies. Requiem Masses and indulgences may shorten the stay. (See *indulgence, Mass.*)

rector See *father.*

rectory A religious house, such as the parsonage (the home of the secular clergy). (See *secular clergy.*)

refectory The dining hall in a monastery.

Requiem Mass See *Mass.*

rosary A series of prayers, including repetitions of the "Hail Mary" and the "Our Father." As he repeats the prayers, the person often keeps count by using a string of beads.

sacerdotal Having to do with the priesthood.

sacrament A religious ceremony supposed to confer grace, or merit with God, upon the recipient. The Catholic church recognizes seven sacraments: Baptism, Confirmation, Eucharist, Penance, Matrimony, Holy Orders (ordination), and Anointing of the Sick, formerly called Last Rites or Extreme Unction. (See *Eucharist, confession.*)

scapular A medal formed of two pieces of woolen cloth joined by strings and worn about the neck. The scapular is supposed to provide protection; if worn at the moment of death, it delivers from Hell.

secular clergy Clergy who serve in the world, as opposed to the "regular clergy," or monastic orders.

Solemn High Mass See *Mass.*

Stations of the Cross A series of meditations on the sufferings of Christ. The number of stations varies, but the most common number is fourteen: (1) Christ's condemnation by Pilate; (2) His carrying of the cross; (3) His first fall; (4) His meeting with His mother; (5) the placing of the cross on Simon; (6) the incident with Veronica's veil; (7) His second fall; (8) His words to the women of Jerusalem; (9) His third fall; (10) the removal of his clothes and the drinking of gall; (11) the crucifixion itself; (12) His death; (13) His removal from the cross; and (14) His burial. Many add a fifteenth, unofficial station, the Resurrection. The stations provide an indulgence if they are accompanied by prayer for the pope. (See *indulgence.*)

tabernacle A box, usually on the altar, that holds the consecrated elements when the mass is not in progress. (See *elements, Mass.*)

transubstantiation See *Mass.*

Vatican II A church council, also called the Second Vatican Council, convened by Pope John XXIII for the purpose of modernizing the church. It met from October 11 to December 8, 1962, and again under Pope Paul VI sporadically from September 29,1963, to December 8, 1965. Its key aim was to prepare the church for the leadership of all world religions in an ecumenical church. To make itself more widely acceptable, it used the Council to appear to give up offensive beliefs and practices without actually doing so.

Bibliography

Abbott, Walter M., S. J. *The Documents of Vatican II.* New York: Guild Press, 1966.

Aquinas, St. Thomas. *On the Truth of the Catholic Faith* (Book I: *God* and Book II: *Creation*). Garden City, N.Y.: Doubleday, 1955.

The Armed Forces Chaplains Board. *Book of Worship for United States Forces.* Washington: Government Printing Office, 1974.

Attwater, Donald. *Dictionary of Saints.* New York: Penguin Books, 1965.

Beach, Bert Beverly. *Vatican II, Bridging the Abyss.* Washington: Review and Herald, 1968.

Berkouwer, Gerrit C. *The Conflict With Rome.* Philadelphia: Presbyterian and Reformed, 1958.

Blanshard, Paul. *Paul Blanshard on Vatican II.* Boston: Beacon Press, 1966.

Brown, Lewis. *This Believing World.* New York: Macmillan, 1930.

Bruce, F.F. *The Spreading Flame.* Grand Rapids: Eerdmans, 1958.

Chiniquy, Charles. *Fifty Years in the Church of Rome.* Grand Rapids: Baker, 1958.

Dillenberger, John. *Martin Luther.* Garden City, N.Y.: Doubleday, 1961.

Dreyer, F.C.H. *Roman Catholicism in the Light of Scripture.* Chicago: Moody, 1960.

Durant, Will. *The Story of Philosophy.* New York: Simon and Schuster, 1953.

Eerdman's Handbook to the History of Christianity. Grand Rapids: Eerdmans, 1977.

Gibbon, Edward. *The History of the Decline and Fall of the Roman Empire.* Boston: Adline, 1940.

Hislop, Alexander. *The Two Babylons, or Papal Worship.* Neptune, N.J.: Loizeaux, 1916.

Kuiper, B.K. *The Church in History.* Grand Rapids: Eerdmans, 1951.

Latourette, Kenneth Scott. *A History of Christianity.* New York: Harper and Row, 1953.

Lehmann, L.H. *Out of the Labyrinth.* Grand Rapids: Baker, 1964.

McGee, J. Vernon. *Genesis,* Vol. 1. Pasadena: Thru the Bible Books, 1975.

——————————. *Revelation,* Vol. 1. Pasadena: Thru the Bible Books, 1975.

McKnight, John P. *The Papacy, A New Appraisal.* New York: Rinehart, 1952.

McLoughlin, Emmett. *American Culture and Catholic Schools.* New York: Lyle Stuart, 1960.

Manhattan, Avro. *Religious Terror in Ireland.* New York: Arno Press, 1972.

——————————. *The Vatican Moscow Alliance.* New York: Ralston-Pilot, 1977.

——————————. *Vatican Imperialism in the Twentieth Century.* Grand Rapids: Zondervan, 1965.

National Geographic Society. *Greece and Rome, Builders of Our World.* Washington: National Geographic Society, 1968.

——————————. *Great Religions of the World.* Washington: National Geographic Society, 1971.

Numers, Ronald L. *Prophetess of Health, A Study of Ellen G. White.* New York: Harper and Row, 1976.

Ott, Ludwig. *Fundamentals of Catholic Dogma.* Rockford, Ill.: Tan Books, 1974.

Pollock, A.J. *Is Roman Catholicism of God?* Lowestoft, England: Green, 1963.

Spence, O. Talmadge. *Charismatism, Awakening or Apostasy?* Greenville, S.C.: Bob Jones University Press, 1978.

Index